Women in the Workplace

Women in the Workplace

Proposals for Research and Policy
Concerning the Conditions of Women in
Industrial and Service Jobs

by

Pamela Roby

SCHENKMAN PUBLISHING COMPANY, INC.
Cambridge, Massachusetts

Copyright © 1981

Schenkman Publishing Company, Inc.
3 Mount Auburn Place
Cambridge, Massachusetts 02138

Library of Congress Cataloging in Publication Data

Roby, Pamela A.
Women in the Workplace.
Includes index.
  1. Women—Employment—United States—Research.
I. Title.
HD6095.R59   331.4′072073   80-24605
ISBN 0-87073-172-6
ISBN 0-87073-173-4 (pbk.)

Printed in the United States of America.

CONTENTS

Page

ACKNOWLEDGMENTS vii

INTRODUCTION 1

SECTION I.   Past and Current Research on
Women in Working-Class Jobs 5

Chapter 1. Research on Women in Blue-Collar, Industrial,
    and Service Jobs: A Review, 1890-1970 7

Chapter 2. Current Research 11
    Womanpower Studies 13
    Women's Liberation Studies 16
    Union Studies 21
    Equal Employment Studies 22
    Vocational Education Studies 23

SECTION II.   Research and Policy Agenda 25

Chapter 3. Wages and Working Conditions 31
    Law Enforcement Processes 31
    Desegregating Work 37
        Job Evaluation 39
        Breaking Into Traditionally Male Jobs 41
    Sex Role Relations and Attitudes on the Job 44
    Health Rights 45
        Working Conditions and Women's Health 45

Government's, Industry's, and Workers'
Perspectives on Women's Health 48
Hours of Work 51
Job Benefits 53
Historical, Demographic, and Ethnographic
Research on Working Conditions 54

Chapter 4. Work, Training, and Promotion Opportunities 57
The Right to Work 58
The Right to Training 61
Vocational Education 61
Apprenticeship Programs 67
Promotion Opportunities 71

Chapter 5. Living conditions 73
Wages 73
Company, Union, and Government Benefits 77
Maternity Policies 77
Childcare Needs 79
Retirement Needs 81
Community Services 83
Attitudes of Husbands 84
Politicizing the Issues 85

Chapter 6. Policies Affecting the Attitudes of
Blue-Collar Employed Women 87

Chapter 7. Unions 91
The Position of Women in Unions 91
Unions and the Enforcement of
Equal Opportunity Laws 94

SECTION III. Conclusion 99
Working Conditions and the U.S. Economy 101
Research Priorities 101

NOTES 103
INDEX 133

ACKNOWLEDGMENTS

Many people helped me write this book. First were the 150 women and men—blue-collar workers, union and government officials, and employers—whom I interviewed. They gave eagerly and warmly of their time and thinking. Many invited me to their homes and workplaces, and all made me feel most welcome. I have tried to transmit their concerns and insights accurately.

Jennifer Hammond and Sara Grisham were research assistants for this project, and Mary Morrison, Carol Beardsley, Judy Burton, and Theresa White typed drafts of the volume. I appreciate the thoughtful care each took with her work.

Jessie Bernard, Sarane Boocock, Arlene Daniels, Andrew Effrat, James Mulherin, Anne Nelson, Sandi Riser, Sharon Walker, Barbara Wertheimer, and several anonymous reviewers read drafts of the volume and gave me both useful suggestions and encouragement.

The Russell Sage Foundation and Ford Foundation provided grants which enabled me to undertake research for and writing of the book. The University of California-Santa Cruz's Academic Senate gave me additional financial assistance; and the Ford Foundation sponsored the First National Working Conference on Research on Women in Blue-Collar Jobs, organized by Barbara Wertheimer, Joyce Kornbluh, and myself. The conference made possible a valuable exchange of information. I am grateful to each institution for its financial assistance; and to Sarane Boocock, Hugh F. Cline, and David Goslin, all formerly of the Russell Sage Foundation, and Susan Berresford and Basil Whiting, of the Ford Foundation, for encouraging me as well.

Pamela Ann Roby
Santa Cruz, California

INTRODUCTION

The number of women employed in blue-collar, industrial, and service jobs is large and growing. Between 1940 and 1979, the number of female salesworkers, craftworkers, operatives, nonfarm laborers, and service workers (except private household) increased from 4.6 to 15.6 million, or 39 percent of the employed women in the United States.[1] Although 46 percent of all employed women of minority races work in these jobs, the vast majority of women (85 percent) employed in these jobs are white.[2]

In 1979 women comprised 42 percent of the employed labor force as compared with 26 percent in 1940; 51 percent of all women 16 years of age and older were part of the labor force.[3] The Department of Labor has reported that most of these women work because they must. In 1978, nearly two-thirds of all women in the labor force either were single, widowed, divorced, separated or had husbands whose annual incomes were less than $10,000 in 1977.[4] Wives' earnings frequently raised families out of poverty. In husband-wife families in 1978, 6.1 percent were poor when the wife did not work; 2.7 percent when she was in the labor force.[5]

Most of these working women had low wages. In 1977, the full-time, year-round (50-52 weeks a year, 35 hours or more a week) median before-tax wage for female operatives was $7,362 ($12,599 for males); for female nonfarm laborers, $7,433 ($10,826 for males); for female salesworkers, $7,098 ($15,798 for males); for female service workers (except private household), $6,431 ($10,354 for males); and for female craftworkers, $8,981 ($14,666 for males).[6]

Over the last fifty years, blue-collar employed women have been largely neglected by researchers and writers. The little research that has been done has focused on how to increase their productivity rather than on how to improve their own and their families' well-being. The purpose of this study is to spark an interest in research and social policies suggested by women employed in blue-collar and service jobs as well as by others who work closely with them. In addition, the conditions and impact of current social policies on blue-collar employed women are outlined to provide a context for understanding the research and policy proposals. Readers who are primarily interested in directions for future research and policy and less concerned with historical and contemporary research should read section II, "Research and Policy Agenda."

The proposed research is needed by government, company, and union policymakers, and by other citizens, in order to make informed decisions concerning working women. It is also necessary for the development of industrial and occupational sociology, women's studies, social welfare, and other disciplines as well as for an understanding of society itself.

Feminist professionals will find that doing research related to the needs of working women is enjoyable as well as valuable. Several doctoral candidates, therefore, might select related topics for their dissertation research. The Society for the Study of Social Problems, Sociologists for Women in Society, and other social science organizations might also help organize teams to undertake research in these areas and generate outside funding. Feminist professional and employed-women's organizations will benefit by working together locally and nationally. Each group can learn skills and gain information from the other. In addition, firm alliances between the two groups are necessary for the liberation of each.

The recently established National Commission on Working Women and Center for Women and Work are a positive step forward. Funded by the National Institute of Education, the Ford Foundation, and the Rockefeller Foundation, the Commission was created to:

- Explore and publicize the problems and needs of women who have low-paying jobs
- Design and carry out action programs to help solve these problems in innovative ways
- Raise public awareness about the status of working women
- Develop policy recommendations concerning the conditions of working women

During the period 1977-78, the Commission held four regional meetings involving hearings and workshops with 100 working women in each. The Commission agreed to focus on the "4 D's" for working women:

- Decent, fair, and equitable wages
- Dignity of work
- Decent work and work-related conditions
- Development of the individual

Although, for purposes of timing, research suggestions are given priority in the concluding chapter, the United States cannot afford to bypass a complete research and action program related to the needs of working women. Not only would doing so be morally indefensible, but the consequent costs of welfare, medical, and other expenses would be many times the cost of the proposed programs.

Readers will find that this volume omits many areas of study. Among these are programs of historical and cross-national research on the conditions of working women and research on the needs and conditions of rural women workers. The impact of women's work on their family relations has been dealt with only briefly here but is the subject of an entire chapter in *Work and Family in the United States* by Rosabeth Kantor.[9] Also omitted are white-collar employed women. The line between the work of women in blue-collar and white-collar jobs is arbitrary. In the mid-1950s, C. Wright Mills noted the similarity of their work: "The new white-collar girl in the centralized transcribing pool cannot know intimately some segment of the office or business, and has lost the private contact that gave status to the secretary and even the stenographer. ... In short, the prized white-collar spot for women is becoming more and more the job of a factory-like operative."[10]

Much research is needed on policies affecting women employed in white-collar jobs. However, this work has been restricted to blue-collar, industrial, and service jobs simply to keep the effort within manageable limits.[11] It does not attempt to develop an overall theory about the conditions of working women. Pursuit of the suggested research will, however, assist in the development of theory as well as policy.[12]

In addition, the following chapters often omit statistical descriptions of the conditions of women who face "double" or "triple" jeopardy because to date the data are nonexistent. Because the liberation of every person is dependent upon the liberation of all persons, we must ensure that governmental agencies in the future provide full information concerning the conditions of ethnic, Third World, young, aged, and handicapped women as well as women who face multiple discrimination.[13]

Finally, policies affecting working women are changing so rapidly that some of those described below will be out of date by the time this volume is published. For this reason, references are provided which enable the reader to keep abreast of particular areas as well as to begin research in those areas.

This study provides a vast amount of useful background information and hundreds of research suggestions made by policymakers and blue-collar women themselves. The following section describes past and current research on women in "working-class" jobs. Chapters in the second section develop research agendas and background information on wages and working conditions; work, training, and promotion opportunities; living conditions; policies affecting the attitudes of blue-collar women; and the status of women in, and the policies of, unions. Conclusions concerning research priorities are contained in the final section.

SECTION I

PAST AND CURRENT RESEARCH ON WOMEN IN "WORKING-CLASS" JOBS

CHAPTER I. RESEARCH ON WOMEN
IN BLUE-COLLAR, INDUSTRIAL, AND
SERVICE JOBS: A REVIEW, 1890-1970

Extensive research on the conditions of women in working-class jobs was conducted between 1900 and 1925. The U.S. Women's Bureau, the Russell Sage Foundation, the Cleveland Foundation, the Consumer's League, and the YWCA all sponsored studies. The nature of their extensive surveys and case studies is reflected in the following sample of book titles:[14]

The Employment of Women in the Clothing Trade
Women and the Labor Movement
A Seasonal Industry: A Study of the Millinery Trade
Italian Women in Industry
Saleswomen in Mercantile Stores
Women as Munition Makers: A Study of Conditions in Bridgeport, Conn.
U.S. Congress, Report on the Condition of Women and Child Wage-Earners in the United States
Mothers in Industry: Wage Earning Women in Philadelphia
Making Both Ends Meet: The Income and Outlay of New York Working Girls
Women Workers in Factories
Legal Recognition of Industrial Women
Mothers Who Must Earn: West Side Studies
Artificial Flower Makers
Women in the Bookbinding Trade
The Food of Working Women in Boston
The Garment Trades

Scores of articles on women workers also appeared in periodicals such as *The Survey, The New Republic, The Nation,* and *The Annals of the American Academy of Political and Social Science.* These books and articles described blue-collar women's working conditions as well as the physical, psychological, and social problems presented by them; living conditions for women and their families; and limited wages for food, housing, and clothing. The books were written for college students, politicians, philanthropists, ministers, and other citizens who could help the women by providing charity or creating social reforms. Written by upper-middle-class and wealthy white Protestant women, most of the books were useful in that they publicized the nature of the women's working and living conditions. The studies, along with much agitation by working people and horrors such as the 1900 New York Triangle Shirtwaist fire, led to the first of reform legislation for working women, namely, the health, fire, and protective laws.[15] However, these reforms, like most of the studies themselves, were limited. Both writers and reformers treated the problems confronting women as isolated phenomena and believed that, given adequate charity and limited government reform, the problems could be remedied and a humane society obtained.[16]

Unlike earlier writers and reformers who blamed the poor for their poverty, these writers blamed company bosses and expected them and the government to rectify the women's working conditions.[17] Both writers and reformers of the early 1920s, however, overlooked the larger inegalitarian social, political, and economic structure in which these and other social problems originated.[18] They failed to address the larger system as they might have otherwise done. Instead they joined with other "progressive" social reformers of their day by replacing the ideological concepts of laissez faire or Darwinian survival of the fittest with, as James Weinstein has aptly observed, an ideal of a liberal, responsible, corporate social order in which all classes would be cared for and "could look forward to some form of recognition and sharing in the benefits of an ever-expanding economy."[19]

The concern about blue-collar working women diminished with the advent of World War I and the general decline of urban social reform. Over the fifty years following 1925, the United States had a notable lack of social science research concerning women in working-class jobs; slippage in many job conditions and five decades of technological change in industrial conditions outdated most previous research. Researchers—sex-role, family, and occupational sociologists; manpower and labor economists; industrial and occupational psychologists; and industrial experts—did not devote a single book primarily to women employed in blue-collar, industrial, or service jobs. Rather, the vast majority of their books, including those intended as "general texts," focused almost exclusively on men.[20] Examples of this type of work are reflected in the titles *Men and Their Work*; *Man, Work, and Society*; *Man in a World at Work*; *Industrial Man*; and *Man, Work, and Organizatins*.

The Hawthorne experiments and other human relations studies of the 1930s and 1940s, which included working-class women as well as men, were aimed primarily at finding means to increase worker productivity rather than to improve workers' employment or living conditions. The studies were conducted by men for other men, the corporate elite who could afford to buy their services.[21] Family sociology texts similarly ignored the existence of working mothers and, in particular, blue-collar working mothers.[22] Mirra Komarovsky's *Blue-Collar Marriage*, researched in the 1950s, is the only exception, and even it devoted only one chapter to the employed blue-collar wife.[23]

Over the last twenty years, occupational and industrial sociologists and other industrial relations researchers who have occasionally mentioned women have given a straightforward account of the occupational distribution of women as compared with men, women's lower wages, and their dual work and family roles. However, many industrial and occupational sociologists have not devoted a single phrase of an entire book to women; those who have done so have given them a few pages or, very occasionally, an isolated chapter. Women are not integrated into discussions of unions, working conditions, vocational choice, work assignment, and alienation. Women's concerns about maternity leave, childcare, the work environment, the process of breaking into traditionally male occupations, fighting for equal pay for equal work, breaking through union barriers, opening up apprenticeships, and other matters discussed below are not mentioned in any of the reviewed occupational or industrial sociology texts. Analyses of what women's wages could buy, as referred to in the literature described earlier, were similarly neglected.

Social science periodicals have also ignored working-class employed women in recent years. The indexes to the *American Journal of Sociology* indicate that this journal published seven articles on employed blue-collar women over an eighty-year period; all seven articles appeared before 1910.[24] In 1943, *The American Sociological Review* published one such article, and the *Sociological Inquiry* had no articles on blue-collar working women until an excerpt from this monograph was published in 1975.[25] Of the 559 papers included in the *Industrial Relations Research Association Proceedings* between 1966 and 1972, several focused primarily on blacks and youth, while most focused on men and none dealt with women or their occupational concerns.[26] Furthermore, women were barely mentioned in any of the twenty papers, all written by men, in the Industrial Relations Research Association's 25th anniversary volume, *The Next Twenty-Five Years of Industrial Relations*, published in 1973.[27]

CHAPTER 2. CURRENT RESEARCH

Recently, there has been a resurgence of interest in women in working-class jobs. Blue-collar women rediscovered their own importance. In 1963, women from the United Automobile Workers and the Communication Workers of America (CWA) were among the founding members of the National Organization for Women. Women held conferences, formed caucuses, and established women's offices in the International Union of Electrical Workers of CWA, the Meatcutters and Butcher Workers, and the AFL-CIO. In 1971, San Francisco women from several unions founded the Union Women's Alliance To Gain Equality (Union WAGE), an organization of working women, including those unemployed, retired, and on welfare, that is dedicated to achieving equal rights, equal pay, and equal opportunities for women on the job, in unions, and in society.[28]

In 1973 and 1974, women from many different trade unions came together to form regional conferences throughout the nation.[29] About the same time, working-class women who were active in the affairs of their communities formed the National Congress of Neighborhood Women. Representatives from Chicago, Detroit, Baltimore, Brooklyn, Florida, and Washington, D.C., included many employed and union women as well as unemployed neighborhood activists. These women pressed for greater educational options and opportunities for working-class women.[30] Then in March 1974, over 3,200 women from fifty-eight national and international unions met in Chicago and formed the Coalition of Labor Union Women (CLUW) to more effectively organize women and encourage unions to be more responsive to the needs of women. Since the national founding conference, women have formed local CLUW chapters throughout the nation.[31]

Industrial and blue-collar women have also shown new militancy at their places of work. Many women have appealed injustices to federal equal employment agencies, while others have mounted demonstrations against the repeal of state protective laws. Still others have valiantly struck for their rights. For nearly two years, for example, women struck Farah pants in El Paso, Texas for the right to form a union.[32] At the same time, Delores Huerta and many other women assumed a vital role in the struggles of the United Farm Workers. In the summer of 1973, over 100 women farmworkers, from teenagers to great-grandmothers, spent weeks in jail for violating antipicket injunctions. By the following summer, women in the long-unorganized northern California electronics industry began to strike for union rights.

The rise of the blue-collar women's rights movement, the rise of the women's liberation movement, and growing national concern with "blue-collar blues" resulting in declining productivity have begun to generate new research on policies affecting women in working-class jobs. Thirty-five researchers and directors of demonstration programs concerned with policies affecting women in blue-collar jobs met for two days in 1974 at a national working conference sponsored by the Ford Foundation. The volume produced by the conference summarizes many of the discussions.[33]

Most recent research reported at the conference and elsewhere has grown out of the researchers' interest in women's liberation in combination with four other major concerns. In the first type of research, manpower concerns have been blended with women's liberation interests. This research has centered on opening training opportunities to women and determining what factors enter into women's decisions to return to work. The second group of research projects stems directly from and builds on new knowledge gained in women's liberation consciousness-raising groups. Some of the research is on the influence of women's employment and women's liberation on the status and power of blue-collar women within their families. Other research asks, in survey form, questions posed in consciousness-raising groups: What are your needs? How do you manage? In the third category of research, union concerns have been combined with women's liberation interests. These researchers have studied how barriers to women's participation in unions can be removed; some have continued to study women's participation in their communities and other organizations. Other researchers in this group, who were also possibly influenced by the health movement, have conducted research through unions on the effect of work on employee health. The fourth and final group of research projects has been motivated by interest in the goals embodied in equal employment legislation.[34]

WOMANPOWER STUDIES

In 1970, Sally Hillsman Baker directed a large-scale sociological study of the operation of selection processes in school and the apparel industry for working-class women.[35] Of these women, who were graduates of a large New York City vocational high school, 28 percent were white, 25 percent were Puerto Rican, and 47 percent were black. The study showed how the school separated the women by race and ethnic background for different levels of work in industry. When they entered the school, black and Puerto Rican students were more frequently assigned to the lower status and less skilled trade groups. This work was primarily garment operating and secondarily dressmaking. White students most frequently entered the "elite" trade of fashion design. Regardless of the trade group in which they were trained, however, minority women more frequently entered the labor market in blue-collar manufacturing jobs (many in the apparel industry) than did their white classmates, who were more likely to be employed in white-collar, nonapparel jobs.[36] Similarly, within apparel manufacturing, white women graduates were, for example, more favorably placed in the generally higher paying, more interesting outerwear industry than black and Puerto Rican women, who were generally placed in other types of firms such as nightwear and undergarments.[37] Baker and Levinson's[38] later analysis of social security earnings data revealed that Puerto Rican and black graduates who pursued the same curriculum as whites earned considerably less, not only upon entry into the labor market but thereafter for the next five years.

An exploratory study, sponsored by the Metropolitan Applied Research Center and directed by Phyllis Wallace, investigated unemployment among black female teenagers in two urban poverty neighborhoods in New York City. This study identified many structural weaknesses in the educational, social service, manpower, and vocational guidance delivery systems' nonresponse to black youth. In addition, it demonstrated the possibilities of providing resources to enable these young women to enter and to take continuing steps to remain in the labor market.[39]

In 1973, the Wisconsin State Employment Service, under the directorship of Norma Briggs and the sponsorship of the Manpower Administration, concluded a multifaceted study of the impact of existing apprenticeship programs on employment opportunities for women. It assessed the demonstration apprenticeship training programs for women and conducted job analyses of occupations typically held by women, which were not included in or were underrated by the *Dictionary of Occupational Titles*.[40] The research suggests many other needed research projects that should be pursued in the near future. These are discussed below along with the study's major findings. In addition, the project produced a color film on women in apprenticeable occupations entitled "Never Underestimate the Power of a Woman," which is available from the Wisconsin Employment Service.

Other action research projects are being carried out. In San Francisco, Advocates for Women, funded in December 1973, places women in apprenticeship programs.[41] In Denver, Better Jobs for Women has been operating since 1971 under the sponsorship of the YWCA and with funding from the Department of Labor. Better Jobs works closely with unions and places women in apprenticeships for high-paying skilled trades, such as auto mechanics, plumbing, carpentry, cabinetmaking, electrical work, cement masonry, tool- and diemaking, truck driving, building, and construction. Sandy Caruthers, director, and Dorothy Haskins, job specialist, speak frequenty to groups of high school and other women in Denver to introduce them to the project and encourage them to consider apprenticeships in high-paying, traditionally male trades. Frequent television spots and other local publicity have further helped the project.[42]

With a grant from the National Institute of Mental Health (NIMH), Mary Lindenstein Walshok, of the University of California at San Diego, has begun to compare the attitudes, training, social backgrounds, and self-images of a cohort of women entering training for nontraditional jobs with a cohort of women entering traditional job training and to evaluate what factors in nontraditional training and work settings lead to various kinds of outcomes for women vis-à-vis the working world.[43]

Several studies stemming directly from manpower and labor force concerns shed light on what work means to women. In 1966, the Parnes nationwide study of women aged 30 to 44 asked, "If, by some chance you (and your husband) were to get enough money to live comfortably without working, do you think that you would work anyway?" Forty-five percent of white as compared with 59 percent of black blue-collar employees and 56 percent of white as compared with 74 percent of black nondomestic service workers said they would work.[44] Although black women expressed more interest in continuing to work in the absence of financial need, when asked, "What would you say is the most important thing about any job—good wages or liking the kind of work you are doing?," black women, perhaps because of greater financial need, more frequently than white women replied, "Good wages."[45] White women more frequently than black, nonmarried more frequently than married, and nondomestic service more frequently than blue-collar employees stated that they were "highly satisfied with their jobs." Considerably more black nondomestic service workers and nonmarried black blue-collar workers than black clerical workers were highly satisfied with their jobs. The reverse was true for white women (see table I).

TABLE 1

PROPORTION OF EMPLOYED RESPONDENTS HIGHLY SATISFIED WITH JOB, BY MARITAL STATUS, OCCUPATION, AND RACE

| | Percent highly satisfied | | Total or average | |
Race and Occupation	Married	Unmarried	Total number (thousands)	Percent
Whites				
White-collar	74	74	4,429	74
Blue-collar	58	52	1,359	57
Nondomestic service	61	69	7,120	68
Total or average*	67	69	7,120	68
Blacks				
White-collar	64	62	363	63
Blue-collar	48	53	264	50
Domestic service			269	
Nondomestic service	62	70	323	65
Total or average**	56	56	1,253	56

*Total includes domestic service and farmworkers not shown separately.
**Total includes farmworkers not shown separately.
Source: Manpower Administration, U. S. Department of Labor, *Dual Careers: A Longitudinal Study of Labor Market Experience of Women*, vol. I. Parnes et al., op. cit., table 6.6, p. 184.

White women appeared more concerned with their job status. Indeed, more white clerical workers earning less than $1.50 per hour (66 percent) than blue-collar workers earning $2.50 or more per hour said they were highly satisfied with their job.[46] When asked what they liked most about their job, "the nature of the work" was the reply most frequently given by white (38 percent) and black (37 percent) blue-collar workers and white (62 percent) and black (53 percent) nondomestic service workers. Wages and coworkers were factors next most frequently cited by white and black blue-collar employees (14 and 12 percent, 12 and 12 percent, respectively).[47]

Few differences have been observed in overall job satisfaction between women and men.[48] Women do, however, appear to be more concerned than men with pleasant and hygienic physical surroundings, convenient hours, and good transportation to and from work.[49]

WOMEN'S LIBERATION STUDIES

The working-class family has been a subject of interest to several researchers, namely, Laura Lein, Lillian Rubin, Mary Lou Finley, Myra Marx Ferree, and Louise Lamphere. With two anthropology, two psychology, and two sociology graduate students, Lein, an anthropologist, recently completed an exploratory indepth study of the actual family arrangements of 14 families in which the mother worked and the total family income was between $8,000 and $13,000. Funded by an NIMH grant, the researchers collected demographic information and diaries from the families and conducted intensive interviews with them. Although the researchers were initially concerned with the childcare arrangements of each family, they broadened the scope of their study to include a wide range of family arrangements.[50] Lein and her colleagues found that many of the couples strongly believed that parents should have sole responsibility for the care and socialization of their children. Several adamantly rejected daycare, while others simply could not afford it. Some of the couples cared for their children without outside help by staggering their work schedules. Others exchanged childcare with neighbors.[51] The researchers were impressed with the difficulties and tensions confronted by working mothers. They reported:

These women constantly encountered (or believe they encounter, which amounts to the same thing) a tacit reproach....

As these women explain it, the working mother is made to feel that she is not only challenging her husband as the breadwinner, but necessarily is neglecting her primary responsibility as homemaker and mother. The psychological pressure of these images and assumptions on the working mother ... are (often) reinforced on a daily basis by her own upbringing, her husband, her relatives, and the wider social environment. Small wonder, then, that so many of the mothers characterize themselves as "nervous," "irritable," "angry," or "short-tempered."

Ambivalence on the part of the husband appeared time and again in our contact with the families. Some of the men justify her employment as supplying supplementary income ... and express their concern about the effect of her absence on the children.[52]

On the brighter side, Lein found that several of the husbands, who cared for their children while their wives were at work, found, to their surprise, that they enjoyed the time spent with the children and that they were skilled in childcare tasks.[53] The researchers were also impressed with the families' resiliency and dignity.[54]

Lillian Rubin, a clinical sociologist, interviewed both wives and husbands of fifty intact white families in the San Francisco Bay area. In the case of each family, the wife was under age forty, at least one child was under age twelve, and neither spouse had more than a high school education. About a third of the wives were employed but considered housewife as their primary occupation. Funded by an NIMH grant, Rubin examined marital conflicts and issues concerning the wives' autonomy within families, how blue-collar wives relate to work outside the home, the attitudes of the men to their wives working, how work is divided in the household, the feelings of wives and husbands about that division of labor, and how conflicts in these areas are resolved.[55]

One of Rubin's first findings was that both husband and wives interviewed were extremely eager to talk with her. Because they had no one else in their lives with whom they could talk about their family conflicts and feelings about their sexual lives, they were often deeply troubled. Consequently, one of Rubin's basic policy recommendations is the provision of a place for people to talk and people to whom they can talk. However, she cautions, "I don't mean to say send in mental health professionals, because they're ... worse than useless. I mean that we need to think about how to train people to talk and do counseling ... I don't care what we call it, with working-class families, because the conflicts are enormous."[56]

Mary Lou Finley, a sociology Ph. D. candidate at the University of Chicago, is studying how women in working-class jobs in Tacoma, Washington perceive their class and sex status as well as the relationship between their work and their home lives. Some of her preliminary observations of major concern to many women are: (1) class and sex-class consciousness may be more prevalent among working-class women than has previously been suspected; (2) there does not appear to be a relationship between consciousness developed at the workplace and consciousness of community and family issues— women with a keen understanding of one area often fail to understand the other at all (further investigation may help to clarify this issue); and (3) many women work under poor health and safety conditions (e.g., roof leaks unrepaired for years, no fans provided in 120-degree rooms, permanent damage to fingers and thumbs caused by processing methods used in canneries).[58]

Myra Marx Ferree, a Ph. D. candidate in the department of psychology and social relations at Harvard, has completed research for her dissertation on what work means to married women who are employed in a nonprofessional capacity outside the home and whose youngest child is in first or second grade. Her sample of 135 mothers was drawn from a working-class Boston area community and consisted of presently married women who had been married for a median of fifteen years. The interviewees had several children (3.4 on the average), had a median age of thirty-six, and were largely high school graduates (57 percent had completed high school, 36 percent had less formal education, and 6 percent had more). Slightly over half the women were employed at the time of their interview—one-third were clerical workers, one-fifth were factory workers, and the remainder were sales and service workers.

Through her interviews, Ferree found that the working-class women with jobs were less alienated and more satisfied than those at home, and that a greater proportion of those housewives who felt a moral obligation to stay at home were more unhappy than those who felt a woman should work if she wants. Sixty percent of the housewives said that they missed something about their jobs as compared with 34 percent of the employed women who said they missed something about being home. Most of the housewives missed contact with other adults; others missed "getting a check with my name on it." The majority of Ferree's total sample expressed support for "efforts to strengthen and change women's status" (80 percent) and for the women's liberation movement (75 percent), and 20 percent volunteered suggestions for ways in which women's status could be improved. Their suggestions included increasing opportunities, improving job conditions (such as providing sick pay for maternity leave), raising children in less sex-stereotyped ways, and changing attitudes about women.

Ferree concluded from these interviews that:

... it is a serious misapprehension to assume that the women's movement is of no consequence to or is opposed by working-class women.

To insist that economics is the only issue on which the movement can speak to poor women is to underestimate both these women and the power of the movement as a whole.

Working-class women generally are not the traditional home-makers of myth. Many work, many others are miserable as housewives. As a consequence, they are also not as disinterested in or repelled by the women's movement as has been assumed.

Though ... financial necessity compels many women to work, they, like their husbands, receive much more than merely financial rewards from the job.

Financial necessity, however, can also be seen as compelling many women to stay home despite their desire for a paid job. As long as women's jobs are so poorly paid that they can scarcely be expected to support a family, husbands hold the power to forbid their wives to seek outside employment. The threat to ... end the marriage is the source of the husband's power within the marriage and this ... is based on the recognition ... that without his income the family would be reduced to poverty. Thus, the real financial necessity faced by working-class women is to get married and stay married. ... Truly equal pay, usually seen only in terms of its consequences for women presently employed, would affect even housewives by changing the consequences of divorce and thus the balance of power within the marriage.[58]

Under a 1976 NIMH Metropolitan Center grant entitled "Women, Work, and Ethnicity in an Urban Setting," anthropologist Louise Lamphere is studying the relationship between work and family roles for working-class women of various ethnic backgrounds who work in semiskilled jobs near Providence, R. I. She is focusing on how women use or are unable to use kin networks for childcare, sharing domestic responsibilities, and exchanging goods and services.[59]

Helena Z. Lopata and other members of the Center for the

Comparative Study of Social Roles at Loyola University in Chicago are studying factors influencing the relative strengths and dimensions of women's changing commitments to a career, an occupation, a job in an organization, working in general, and earning an income. The first phase of the study involved interviews with 1,000 Chicago area women aged twenty-five to fifty-four, while the second phase will expand the sample into a national base. The study, "Changing Commitment of Women to Work and Family Roles," is funded through a contract with the Social Security Administration.[60]

In 1972, Social Research, Inc., of Chicago, surveyed a sample of working-class women drawn from eight cities. It found that the women were less home-bound and more active in the local community and more assertive within their homes than a similar sample in 1959. Nearly all the respondents also endorsed the idea of allowing any woman to hold any job for which she has the necessary work skills and qualifications.[61]

Nancy Seifer's *Absent from the Majority: Working-Class Women in America* is a general account of the status and concerns of employed and unemployed working-class women. Her report, unlike that of Social Research, Inc., contains numerous social policy recommendations.[62] More recently, Seifer published *Nobody Speaks for Me!*, in which ten American working-class women tell of their neighborhood and workplace organizing experiences.[63]

Under an NIMH grant, Rachelle Warren has examined the helping resources used by blue-collar employees (females, 37; males, 153) as compared with samples of white-collar employees (females, 97; males, 161). She found that a wide range of support systems differ according to both the sex and the occupational level of the employed individual. A spouse's help in problem solving was used to a greater extent by both blue- and white-collar male workers than by female workers. Blue-collar employed women tended to rely more heavily on their relatives than did other groups of employees. Blue-collar men relied significantly more on their coworkers for help with their problems than did blue-collar employed women, although there was little difference based on sex among white-collar workers. White-collar employed women relied considerably more on friends than did the other groups. They were also the most likely to use formal agency helpers (e.g., doctors, clergy, police, teachers, counselors); the blue-collar employed women were least likely to use these helpers, although they relied more heavily on the clergy than did the others.[64] Moreover, Warren found that blue-collar individuals, women in particular, were confronted by a greater number of problems.

Several women are studying blue-collar women's issues under Ford Foundation study-travel grants. Alice Cook is completing an international study of how women in blue-collar and industrial jobs cope and what they most need. She found that childcare fitted to their work schedules was the assistance most wanted by mothers around the world. When they could not find childcare assistance, mothers sought part-time work geared to their children's school day and calendar.[65] Under another Ford Foundation grant, Louise Kapp Howe recently authored *Pink-Collar Worker*, a book of case studies about the work and lives of waitresses, salespersons, and women in banking.[66]

UNION STUDIES

There is little documentation on the lives of women in working-class jobs and women labor leaders today. Nearly all oral histories of union leaders have been about men or their wives. With funding from the Rockefeller Foundation, Joyce Kornbluh, Robin Jacoby, and Marilyn Young, of the University of Michigan, are beginning an oral history project in which they will interview trade union women who have organized for union recognition, job security, better working conditions, improved childcare, and equal rights in an effort to correct this important gap in our knowledge.[67]

Barriers to the participation of women in New York unions were studied in 1973 by Barbara Wertheimer and Anne Nelson under a Ford Foundation grant. The study involved a survey of the distribution of women in ninety-two New York City locals, their leadership positions, and the attitude of union leadership toward female members' job and union advancement. The study also contained indepth action research with seven diverse New York locals, most of which had a predominantly female membership and predominantly male top leadership.[68] The survey found that when women comprised a sizable proportion of their union's membership, their general participation was higher and they were more willing to run for office. The indepth study found that participation at every level of union activity is jeopardized by lack of information, training, and experience on the part of most women, and not by lack of interest. The study also showed that women are barred from leadership roles by the preconceptions about the role of women held by many men in both leadership and rank-and-file positions.

The project included monthly luncheon seminars with New York women trade union leaders on issues of concern to union women. Wertheimer and Nelson are now experimenting with the development of optimal educational programs to meet the training and informational needs of trade union women.

Chemist Jeanne Stellman, chief of the Division of Occupational Health and Toxicology of the American Health Foundation, is concerned with the effect of work on women's health and will soon be surveying women in a variety of blue-collar jobs about their health problems. She has recently published an excellent, highly readable, and well-documented introductory text on women's occupational health entitled *Women's Work, Women's Health*.[69]

Sociologist Patricia Sexton, another recipient of a Ford Foundation study-travel grant as well as a Department of Labor contract, is interviewing working-class women to identify their problems, dissatisfactions, and satisfactions at home, on the job, and in the community. She is particularly concerned with their organizational participation and alienation.[70]

EQUAL EMPLOYMENT STUDIES

Mary Stevenson, of the University of Michigan, reports in her economics dissertation about tests she has made of theories on why women have low-paying jobs. She found that "equal pay for equal work," though important, is only a small part of the larger question of why women workers receive low wages. Sex segregation in labor markets is, she concluded, "the real problem underlying the low wages that women receive. It would seem that whenever women are cordoned off into a circumscribed number of occupations and industries, the consequences are low wages."[71]

There is no evidence that the clustering of women in specific occupations is only a matter of access and social influence. Information is not available on what proportion of women, if given a real opportunity, would choose to move into traditionally male jobs. All the information suggests, however, that given a real choice, women would move into every level of the industrial hierarchy.[72] Indeed, Janice Hedges and Stephen Bemis have reported that between 1960 and 1970, when some doors were opened to women, the rate of increase of women in the skilled trades was eight times the rate for men.[73]

Under the sponsorship of the Equal Employment Opportunity

Commission (EEOC), sociologist Judy Long-Laws examined the structure and operation of sexism and racism within the American Telephone & Telegraph Co. (A.T. & T.) She found that workers were divided into different job categories, first by sex and then by race.[74]

The A.T. & T. is now initiating several studies to aid in the implementation of the affirmative action program, agreed to under a 1972 consent decree. The primary focus of this research is to identify barriers for women moving to and successfully remaining in traditionally male, blue-collar craft jobs and to develop programs to overcome these barriers. Brigid O'Farrell, working with a company of the Bell Telephone System, is focusing on identified recruitment and training needs. Currently, this includes an attitude study of 360 nonmanagement women in traditional and nontraditional blue-collar jobs, a technical job study with emphasis on formal and informal training, and an intensive training program to develop female role models in the foreperson position.[75]

VOCATIONAL EDUCATION STUDIES

In 1975, the author completed a review of the status of women in vocational education and of major research projects related to women in vocational education.[76] Little of the multimillion-dollar funding for vocational education research and development has been devoted to concerns related to the status of women.[77] Nonetheless, the few projects that have been funded are important to women who will eventually be employed in working-class jobs. The demonstration research project on "Equal Vocational Education" at Sam Houston High School in Houston, Texas directed by Joseph Champagne, serves as a model for all high schools. This school not only recruits females into vocational programs that have traditionally been dominated by males, but also maintains the increased female enrollment in these courses.[78]

Other important programs should also be mentioned. Under funding by the state of Illinois, JoAnn Steiger is developing and testing curriculum materials to encourage girls to consider a wider range of jobs.[79] In addition, Jacob Kaufman and Morgan Lewis are attempting to identify any common factors or conditions that appear to be essential for the establishment of nontraditional programs for young women, by locating and comparing ten successful vocational education programs in secondary schools that prepare young women for occupations traditionally considered appropriate only for males.[80]

The research described above provides useful insights concerning the conditions of women employed in blue-collar jobs. A very small fraction of the thousands of research projects, however, is currently being conducted and funded by the U. S. government and various foundations. More important, the research conducted to date has only begun to touch on the conditions, needs, problems, and concerns of the 13 million women employed in blue-collar jobs that require the attention of researchers and policymakers today.

SECTION II

RESEARCH AND POLICY AGENDA

INTRODUCTION

Why should social science research be devoted to blue-collar employed women and their families? First, research is needed to help policymakers gain a better understanding of how to meet the needs of these women and their families. Second, and equally important, social scientists who study the conditions of a group of people generally act on its behalf in several ways. Their research and writing focus public attention on the group's needs. As "experts" on the group or some aspect of its life, the scientists also informally lobby for the group as well as give "expert" testimony on its behalf. Moreover, the researchers help individuals or subgroups within the study group to recognize clearly their own needs, to interpret laws and other aspects of the system, and to change the system to meet their needs. The many social scientists who have been funded to do research on blue-collar men and white-collar men and women have frequently acted on behalf of these groups in the ways described above. For the last 50 years, blue-collar women have not had this assistance.[81]

The research proposed in this text is directed toward the creation of social policies to improve the living conditions of women employed in blue-collar jobs and of their families. The suggested research is oriented toward determining what social policies need to be maintained, abolished, or created. In addition, where specific social policies have already been suggested by previous research, the establishment and implementation of these policies, coupled with evaluation research, will be recommended. Similarly, where policies have been formally established but then partially or totally neglected, their full implementation, done through evaluation research, will be recommended.

Research should precede policymaking, policy implications should be considered at every step of research, and evaluation research should accompany the implementation of social policies. Because research, policymaking, and action should be closely intertwined, it is difficult to separate recommendations for each. The following sections are therefore divided according to issues that affect the lives of blue-collar employed women, and each section contains clearly differentiated proposals for research, policy, and action.

In the past, many social policies have suffered consequences unintended by those who proposed them. For example, protective and hours laws for women have resulted in employers using the laws to justify their refusal to employ women or to pay them equal wages. In the following sections, disadvantages as well as advantages of various policy proposals are discussed. Researchers who pursue studies suggested below should consider, examine, and describe the difficulties as well as the benefits that may be derived from the proposed policies. Persons conducting demonstration research should seek to uncover potential unintended consequences of their policy proposals. For the research proposed here to have a greater impact than most research of the past, U.S. government granting agencies and foundations should experiment with allocating funds so that researchers can disseminate their findings to the concerned public, relevant policymakers, and social change agents through television and newspaper interviews, speaking engagements, and other means.

Due to the development and increasing sophistication of applied sociology and the study of political economy over the past decade, researchers who pursue the studies described below are less likely to be guilty of the "fallacy of the middle range" than were their predecessors. In the early 1900s, researchers had concentrated on particular problems confronting women in working-class jobs and did not relate the problems to their origins in the larger social, economic, and political system. Instead, policy-oriented research and reform efforts are likely to be directed toward obtaining fundamental as well as incremental change.

Reforms or incremental changes may facilitate fundamental change by alleviating highly oppressive conditions (e.g., 60-hour workweeks) that prevent blue-collar women from devoting time to activities as well as merely trying to survive. The process of working to obtain these incremental reforms may be directed toward more fundamental change by educating people in the skills of organizing for social change, by helping people take 'charge of their own lives and environment rather than passively accepting whatever comes their way, and by conceptually linking social problems to their roots in the larger political and economic system. In addition, research related to reform efforts may be directed toward more fundamental change by making people aware of their needs, giving them a model of the specific benefits that should be obtained from an egalitarian, life-enhancing society, and sharing examples of successful persons who have acted collectively to fulfill their needs.

Most of the following research recommendations were suggested by 150 blue-collar employed women and union, company, government, and organizational officials, primarily women who make or are concerned with policies affecting women; they were interviewed in major cities of the west coast, east coast, and Midwest. Other recommendations evolved from discussions with these individuals through tours of numerous factories and other workplaces.

The research and policy proposals fall into five major categories:

(1) Wages and working conditions

(2) Opportunities for work, training, and upward occupational mobility

(3) Government, company, and union policies affecting conditions of living off the job

(4) Policies affecting the attitudes and consciousness of women

(5) Unionization and union policies and practices

The setting of research priorities in these various areas is discussed in section III.

CHAPTER 3. WAGES AND WORKING CONDITIONS

LAW ENFORCEMENT PROCESSES

Since 1963, federal and state governments have passed several laws and created executive orders prohibiting discrimination against women in the labor force. The Equal Pay Act passed by Congress in 1963 and administered by the Wage and Hour Division of the Department of Labor states that men and women who perform "equal work" must receive equal wages. Enforced by the Equal Employment Opportunity Commission (EEOC), Title VII of the Civil Rights Act of 1964 prohibits sex discrimination in the hiring, promotion, training, layoff, and discharge policies of employers, employment agencies, unions, and hiring halls with fifteen or more employees. Executive Order 11246, issued by President Lyndon B. Johnson in 1965 and amended in 1967 by Executive Order 11375, forbids discrimination against women in companies contracted with the federal government; this order is administered by the Office of Federal Contract Compliance of the Department of Labor. Most states have fair employment laws forbidding sex discrimination in employment; a few states have protective laws for women that conflict with Title VII of the Civil Rights Act, which states that men and women must be treated equally in employment. What these laws cover and how to file complaints under them are clearly summarized in *A Working Woman's Guide to Her Job Rights*, published by The Women's Bureau, Department of Labor.[82]

The processes by which these laws are enforced and can be improved deserve extensive and careful study from a number of perspectives.[83] Evaluation research should be conducted by responsible federal offices. It should specify the companies' progress toward their stated affirmative action goals and answer the following questions: What affirmative action plans have worked for women blue-collar, industrial, and service workers? Why? (One might highlight the companies that have done an outstanding job of assuring that women are treated justly.) Which and how many industries are not meeting the federal affirmative action requirements? What is being done about them?

The procedures for filing and completing complaints should be studied. What barriers prevent women from filing or carrying through on complaints under each of the laws? To what extent have unionized and nonunionized blue-collar women been made aware of the existence of the laws? What is involved in filing a complaint—must they make long-distance phone calls or take time off from their jobs to file? To what extent do union stewards help women file complaints? What attitudes do government officials display toward the women who make complaints? Are the government offices open during periods when women can make complaints, or only during their working hours? What additional staffing is needed in affirmative action offices to provide adequate outreach and compliance programs for blue-collar women? What followup has occurred after decisions have been made in favor of complainants?

One EEOC compliance officer has maintained that the weakest point in the EEOC process is the limited followup after an investigation has been held and a compliance ruling has been made with a company or union. Decisionmaking within EEOC and other compliance agencies, involving both the phases of the compliance process receiving priority and the nature of the individual complaints receiving priority, should be studied.[84] Do complaints of professionals receive priority over those of blue-collar workers? Inadequate staffing may cause weaknesses in the enforcement of EEOC and other equal employment laws, which have been frequently amended to cover additional categories of employees without accompanying increments in staff.

The Civil Rights Act of 1964 states that sex discrimination investigations shall be initiated only by citizen complaints. In contrast, the Equal Pay Act, which is limited to equal pay considerations, allows investigations to be initiated by the Wage and Hour Division when there is reason to suspect a violation of the law. The Equal Pay Act may therefore cover women who show inability or reluctance to initiate a complaint, while the Civil Rights Act does not.

Pay levels and promotion rates should be monitored regularly and automatically by federal agencies at the level of the firm without the necessity of citizen complaints. Toward this end, Congress should amend Title VII of the Civil Rights Act to direct the EEOC to regularly launch its own investigations. Currently, among the categories of employees still unprotected under the Equal Pay Act are those of small retail and service establishments composed primarily of women.

It is also important to explore judges' knowledge of and attitudes toward the new laws on women's employment rights. What percentage of the judges and other officials who make decisions on female employee complaints are women? Dorothy Haener, an international representative of the United Automobile Workers and an advocate of women's issues, recommends that a book be published on court, EEOC, and Wage and Hour Division decisions regarding working women and affirmative action inservice training of employment service personnel, judges, court commissioners, and public prosecutors.

Linda Tarr-Whelan, former deputy director for the program development of the American Federation of State, County, and Municipal Employees and national secretary of the Coalition of Labor Union Women (CLUW), urges the federal government to investigate the kind of legislation that could restore the protective laws that have been rescinded over the last decade. The extent to which equality of law has been achieved through abolishing protections for women rather than extending them to men should also be explored.[85] A major question is to what extent women have been treated unequally by being given the heaviest or dirtiest jobs by forepersons who resent their presence. Although the EEOC has ruled against this type of treatment,[86] a large-scale survey of women in blue-collar, industrial, and service jobs should be conducted to determine the pervasiveness of this type of treatment and means of coping with it.

High-quality muckraking research is needed to uncover and document the many sewing and other industrial operations that illegally employ thousands of women. These companies make no effort to obey minimum wage and other laws and exploit poor immigrant women who know neither English nor minimal employment norms.

To undertake the recommended research projects, several recent federal evaluations of civil rights enforcement practices should be read and analyzed. *The Federal Civil Rights Enforcement Effort—1974*, published by the U.S. Commission on Civil Rights, evaluated the civil rights activities of the regulatory agencies, the Federal Communications Commission (FCC), the Interstate Commerce Commission, the Civil Aeronautics Board, the Federal Power Commission, and the Securities and Exchange Commission. It reported that:

> ... although the regulatory agencies are charged with overseeing significant sectors of the American economy in the public interest, with the exception of the FCC none of the agencies have acknowledged responsibility for ... eliminating employment discrimination in the industries they regulate.
>
> While the Federal Communications Commission has adopted rules prohibiting its licensees from discriminating in their employment practices, its enforcement program has been highly inadequate. FCC's guidelines defining the elements of the affirmative action programs required of licensees lack specificity and are not result oriented. The agency's handling of employment discrimination complaints is also inadequate. License renewal reviews of radio and television stations' employment patterns are used to identify licensees with severe underutilization of minorities and women, but the criteria used to identify these stations are overly restrictive and ignore several important factors.[87]

The General Accounting Office (GAO) in 1975 published a report on federal efforts to end job discrimination, *The Equal Opportunity Program for Federal Nonconstruction Contractors Can Be Improved.* Its investigation focused on the enforcement of Executive Order 11246 described earlier in this chapter. As Representative Richard Bolling, chairperson of the Subcommittee on Fiscal Policy of the Joint Economic Committee, has stated:

> The Labor Department and the compliance agencies have one of the most powerful enforcement tools available—cancellation of federal contracts—to bring about an end to job discrimination. The Federal government lets over $50 billion in contracts every year, and with the power of the Executive Order behind it, the Labor Department could make job equality a reality in many of the Nation's largest corporations. Yet, GAO found the Federal enforcement efforts riddled with inefficiencies.
>
> Executive Order 11246 was issued 10 years ago, yet the Labor

Department's Office of Contract Compliance, charged with enforcing the order, still doesn't have a means for evaluating the progress of Federal contractors. ... The Labor Department can't claim success or failure in ending job discrimination because it hasn't yet developed measures to assess job gains of women and Blacks. ... Most of the compliance agencies that operate under the Labor Department do not even have a complete list of the contractors for whom they are responsible. Furthermore, the Labor Department, which is charged with overseeing the compliance efforts in different agencies, has evaluated one of the thirteen agencies since 1972. Nor are the compliance agencies entirely blameless for the failure of the contract compliance program. GAO found that 20 percent of the Affirmative Action plans approved by the Department of Defense don't meet Federal guidelines. In the General Services Administration, ... GAO investigators found that 70 percent of the Affirmative Action plans approved were deficient and did not have sufficient safeguards to bring about job equality. Most agencies were reviewing only a small number of contractors. In some cases they were reviewing contractors with employees of 50 or less rather than checking large companies where the opportunities for job gains among women and Blacks are greatest. Many compliance agencies were reluctant to take any action against contractors. Although a number of contractors have failed to comply with Federal guidelines, only one contractor has even had a contract terminated for non-compliance with the program.[88]

The GAO report recommended that the secretary of labor should:

- Accelerate implementation of a system to measure progress of nonconstruction contractors and to assess program short-comings in increasing and advancing minorities and women in the work force
- Place greater emphasis on monitoring the nonconstruction program
- Provide adequate and timely guidance to compliance agencies, especially in areas where agencies have requested assistance to perform more complete compliance reviews
- Establish training courses for compliance officers

- Sample and review the compliance of approved affirmative action plans with Department guidelines and fully document results of these reviews
- Require compliance agencies to take timely enforcement action against contractors who do not comply with the Executive order
- Assist compliance agencies to better identify contractors under each agency's responsibility
- Perform periodic tests to determine whether compliance agencies make pre-award reviews and whether contracting agencies request pre-award clearance when appropriate
- Coordinate with the Commission at headquarters and regional levels and make periodic tests to ensure that compliance data on file with the Commission are considered by compliance agencies during reviews and that information is exchanged to minimize duplication of effort[89]

In 1977, Eleanor Holmes Norton, chairperson of the EEOC, outlined a plan to reorganize all federal equal employment programs under the EEOC. This plan was approved by President Jimmy Carter in 1978. According to Norton, the chief purpose of the reorganization was "to improve the enforcement of Title VII."[90] Under the plan, EEOC assumed responsibility for:

- Developing substantive equal employment standards applicable to the entire federal government
- Standardizing federal data collection procedures
- Creating joint training programs
- Establishing requirements to ensure that information is shared among the enforcement agencies
- Developing governmentwide complaint and compliance review methods[91]

Proposed consolidations and transfers under the plan would reduce the number (from 15 to 3) of federal agencies having important equal employment opportunity responsibilities under Title VII and federal contract compliance provisions.[92]

In 1977, EEOC also introduced an internal reorganization plan including:

- A new, rapid case-processing system with emphasis on expanded intake procedures, face-to-face factfinding, and settlement
- A separate backlog case-processing system to give systematic and priority attention to presently backlogged cases
- A "direct service," consumer-oriented structure patterned after the National Labor Relations Board
- Integration of litigation, investigation, and conciliation functions
- Establishment of a program to deal with systemic discrimination, addressing first those whose actions have demonstrated clear disregard for the purpose of Title VII
- A new program office to place the Commission in an affirmative posture for developing Title VII through guidelines, interpretations, and other rulings
- A new management accountability and information system to ensure that the above programs are implemented
- A national training program and standards to ensure that the EEOC staff will be able to administer the new systems effectiveness

After introducing the above plan, EEOC issued proposed guidelines on voluntary affirmative action under which the Commission would find no violation of Title VII if an employer conducts a self-analysis of his employment system; has a reasonable basis for concluding that it might be held in violation of Title VII; and takes voluntary, remedial, or affirmative action "reasonably calculated to avoid that result." Under the proposed guidelines, both public and private employers would be obligated to comply without waiting for government or court action.[94]

The effectiveness of the new federal enforcement procedures outlined above will need to be monitored and researched over the coming years. The questions and problems raised earlier concerning the enforcement of Title VII should be kept in mind by researchers investigating the new plans.

DESEGREGATING WORK

When one hears the term "female ghetto," the secretarial pool usually comes to mind. However, in industry hundreds of jobs are filled only by women and minorities, while the better-paying jobs go solely to men. In the sewing divisions of auto industries, for example, women and black men have the hard, heavy, lower-paid jobs involved in sewing and lifting upholstery. White men have the lighter, higher- paid jobs, such as guiding automated cutting machines, changing sewing machine parts, and driving tractors onto which women and black men load upholstery. Similarly, in the textile mills, where the pay differential is considerable, loomfixers are men and loomtenders are women. In the garment industry, women sew and men cut. Cutters and sewers within the same plant belong to separate union locals. Despite the federal laws against sex discrimination, industrial employers interviewed had replied openly, "We always keep the women and men separate." Workers in their plants defined "separate" as meaning lower pay for women.

In addition to sex segregation in factories, female hospital aides and other service workers have segregated jobs in hospitals and other public institutions. Although the impact on women's wages and opportunities is known, too little attention has been paid to the many sex-segregated jobs. Elizabeth Waldman and Beverly McEaddy have reported that women, like men, find jobs in the fastest growing industries. Waldman and McEaddy report, for example:

> In January 1973, most industries paying average weekly earnings of less than $100 were female-intensive. Several were paying under $90 a week, while the weekly paycheck for all industries averaged $138. The average salary for all manufacturing workers was $159 a week in January 1973. For those in manufacturing industries that were female-intensive, the average was much lower—for example the apparel industry in which 81 percent of the employees were women, paid average weekly salaries of only $93.[95]

Although women have recently broken into the higher-paying skilled trades in greater numbers, the percentage of women workers in these jobs remains small. For example, only 1.8 percent of women workers over age sixteen were employed in craft and kindred jobs in 1979.[96] Social discrimination rather than aptitude has barred women from these skilled jobs. Extensive studies by the Human Engineering Laboratory of the Johnson O'Connor Research Foundation show that many women have the aptitudes to perform jobs that have been dominated by men. In fact, the research indicates that no significant sex difference exists in fourteen of the aptitude and knowledge areas studied, and of the remaining areas, men excel in two and women in four.[97]

Thorough examination of the problem of sex-segregated jobs will illuminate the means of alleviating the problem. Two possible solutions, job evaluation and assistance to women breaking into traditionally male jobs, will be discussed in detail below.

Job Evaluation

The Wage and Hour Division has interpreted the Equal Pay Act to mean that women need not perform exactly the same job as men for their work to be considered equal to that of men. Rather, the act states, "Insubstantial or minor differences in the degree or amount of skill, or effort, or responsibility required for the performance of jobs will not render the equal pay standard inapplicable."[98]

Since the passage of the Equal Pay Act and other women's employment rights legislation, many job categories have simply been changed from "male and female" to "heavy and light," although the "light" jobs are often heavier than the "heavy" jobs. This evasive tactic for maintaining wage inequalities ("heavy" jobs pay more) is illegal but goes unchallenged unless a woman files a complaint. Similarly, women and men who perform the same job often have different job titles. Often, for example, women are called "electronics assemblers" and men, "electronics technicians." The job is the same, but "electronics assemblers" receive lower pay. These situations must be unveiled and challenged.

Another source of wage inequality, the rating of expertise, needs to be investigated. More often men have gained their experience through formal schooling while women have gained job-relevant knowledge or expertise equal to that of men though on-the-job experience, yet women are paid lower wages and have a smaller chance for promotion. Ruth Weyand, associate general counsel of the International Union of Electrical, Radio and Machine Workers, has pointed out that in electronics plants, women assemblers, many who have been on the job for thirty years, often have a better understanding of electronics than male engineers with university educations. In some hearing aid plants, women perform wiring and etching with the aid of a microscope. This job takes weeks to learn and pays less than that of a janitor.[99] Women workers in most plants claim that a woman can train two or three men for jobs of higher position without being considered for those positions and sometimes not considering them herself.

To date, industrial jobs held primarily by women have not been evaluated to determine how many of these jobs are considered equal to those held primarily by men unless a woman makes a complaint.[100] All enforcement of the labor force equal rights laws therefore depends on women making complaints. Only a small fraction of the existing wage inequalities, however, are brought to the attention of the Wage and Hour Division for the following reasons:

- Women working in one type of job seldom speak about their wages with men working in different but similar types of jobs in another part of a plant.
- Women generally do not realize that they can make complaints under the Equal Pay Act about unequal pay for substantially equal rather than identical work.
- Women hesitate to file complaints even when aware of the consequences of not doing so.

Although job evaluations are not routinely conducted in plants, ten state job analysis field centers under supervision of the Department of Labor continuously conduct a massive number of job evaluations to be issued in the *Dictionary of Occupational Titles* (D.O.T.). Job analysis itself has been a sex-segregated job performed by only a few women; consequently, the State of Wisconsin Occupational Analysis Project found in 1975 that a sample of jobs traditionally held by women were not only underpaid but also underrated in terms of complexity in the D.O.T. Those jobs could accurately be rated much higher by using the existing D.O.T. guidelines. In addition, many other jobs traditionally held by women were not rated in the D.O.T.

Following the recommendations of the Wisconsin Occupational Analysis Project, in 1977 the Department of Labor issued the D.O.T. for the first time in twelve years and expunged references to sex and age in job titles and descriptions (e.g., the term "draftsman" was changed to "drafter"). Nevertheless, the 1977 edition still appeared to contain built-in biases in its job skill ratings in favor of jobs held traditionally by men. For example, jobs of newspaper carriers and parking lot attendants, which are filled predominantly by men, were rated higher in "skill and complexity" than those of home health aides, who care for elderly, convalescent, or handicapped persons in the patient's home; nursery school teachers, who instruct "children in activities designed to promote social, physical, and intellectual growth"; and private duty nurses.

Job analysis is needed throughout private industry and public institutions to uncover sex discrimination in wages. This undertaking will require some limited but important refinements in the D.O.T. job analysis guidelines. Mary Witt, senior research analyst of the Wisconsin Occupational Analysis Field Center, has recommended that guidelines be developed for rating "intuitive intelligence." She has also recommended that a study be made on how the D.O.T. is used and on what improvements could be suggested by the users. Although the D.O.T. states in an opening paragraph that it may not be used for setting wages, it is indeed widely used for this purpose.[101] For example, Norma Briggs has discovered that the Wisconsin Civil Service Classification and Compensation Plan classifies jobs and pay according to the D.O.T.'s classification level. She reports that:

> . . . a beginning typist was rate one and hired at $432 a month in 1973. A beginning stock clerk or shipping and mailing clerk was rate four on the blue-collar scale and hired at $141 more per month ($573.33). A Licensed Practical Nurse at rate six on the scale of technical workers is paid precisely what a parking attendant and motor vehicle operator (rate five of the blue-collar scale) are paid.[102]

Breaking Into Traditionally Male Jobs

Job analysis research and equalizing pay for equal work is one answer to sex-segregated work. However, as suggested earlier by Mary Stevenson, there may always be a tendency for men's jobs to pay more than women's jobs as long as they remain segregated. In addition, some women are discovering that they prefer jobs traditionally held by men. Therefore, ways must be developed for women to break more quickly and easily into jobs traditionally held by men.[103]

Gloria Johnson, director of the women's department of the International Union of Electrical Workers, tells of incidents when men supported women who moved into traditionally male jobs.[104] Women steelworkers, who have recently broken into jobs that were held only by men since World War II, have reported that black men, perhaps sensitized by their own experiences of fighting discrimination, have helped them learn their new jobs while white men have often harassed them and refused to teach them even basic safety precautions. This harassment included foremen forcing women during their probationary period to carry excessive weights normally carried by tractors; male workers refusing to teach women safety precautions, which were always taught to new men; men telling women, "You wanted the job, now you can cope with it"; and foremen refusing to grant normal breaks and assigning them jobs ordinarily performed by two men. This treatment of women resulted in physical injury; quitting the job or being fired; gritting their teeth and keeping their jobs; or organizing other women, filing union complaints, or suing the companies.

Clearly, studies on the experiences of women who are moving into traditionally male jobs are needed to identify male attitudes and harassment that other women who break into new job areas will need to combat. Herbert Meyer and Mary Dean Lee have recently completed a study on women who entered traditionally male white-collar as well as blue-collar jobs in selected public utility companies. The study found that because many women felt the need to prove themselves and be accepted by men, they had to do more work than would have been required of a man. Few blue-collar women felt that the key to their success was the supervisor's positive attitude.[105]

Before entering nontraditional jobs, women should first become familiar with problems that may be encountered, how to cope with those problems, and how to form better relationships with their supervisors. A book containing this information could usefully be published and accompanied by training and consciousness-raising conferences for women. Forepersons, union stewards, and workers in traditionally male job areas could be given human relations sensitivity training to prepare them for women working in their traditionally all-male divisions or shops. Men and women in traditionally male departments might also be brought together in joint problem-solving meetings held during working hours.

These inservice training or consciousness-raising sessions should include efforts to discover and deal with men's fears about women entering traditionally male jobs. The many men—young and old, black and white—who willingly assist women in learning traditionally male jobs might be involved in leading these sessions. Stewards, foremen, and workers who actively assist women in breaking into new jobs should be rewarded with bonuses just as they would be if they performed some other aspect of their job especially well. The young, college-educated "blue jeans" women have considerable confidence and choose to work in a plant rather than an office because they feel that this is the only way to keep "body and soul" together. These women may be pioneers by helping other women break into the traditionally male jobs.

Careful evaluation should accompany all suggestions proposed above and be used as a guide for modifying and constructing new proposals to help women break into jobs traditionally closed to them. In March 1976, the U.S. Supreme Court ruled that individual blacks and women who were denied jobs in violation of Title VII of the Civil Rights Act of 1964 must be awarded seniority once they succeed in obtaining those jobs. The ruling is likely to support the concepts of affirmative action and women's right to enter jobs traditionally held by men.[106] In addition, the National Commission on the Observance of International Women's Year has asked the Office of Federal Contract Compliance of the Department of Labor to issue instructions that hiring goals for women be included in all hometown construction plans, such as the Philadelphia Plan and Washington, D.C.'s subway project, either initially or during renegotiation. Following the recommendation, the U.S. Department of Labor issued regulations relating to construction work in April 1978. The regulations set a nationwide goal of having women hold 6.9 percent of all construction industry jobs by March 31, 1981 and outlined specific affirmative steps that employers who have more than $10,000 in federal or federally assisted construction contracts must take to show a good faith effort to achieve goals for women. These include increasing their applicant flow of women for consideration for employment; maintaining a working environment free of harassment, intimidation, and coercion at all sites and in all facilities where employees work; where possible, assigning two or more women to each construction project; and developing on-the-job programs for the area which expressly include women. Some employers maintain that there are simply not enough women interested in construction jobs and jobs directly related to construction to meet the 6.9 percent goals. The San Francisco based Tradeswomen, Incorporated and other women's organization dispute the employers' claim and state that as yet adequate procedures and funding have not been developed to reach out and inform women about the jobs.[107]

SEX ROLE RELATIONS AND ATTITUDES ON THE JOB

A primary concern of many women workers is to gain respect on the job from bosses and fellow workers. Equal, adequate wages and good working conditions are, of course, part of that respect, but much more stems directly from the attitudes of bosses and others. The following might be considered: How do foremen respond when a woman requests to leave the line to go to the restroom or make a phone call? How do bosses and stewards respond to suggestions or complaints from women as compared with men? To what extent do foremen expect presents and sexual favors from women workers in exchange for decent working conditions? How much does a waitress lose in tips if she does not flirt with male customers?

Bitsy Gomez, founder of the Los Angeles Coalition of Women Truck Drivers, reports that most women who have joined the coalition complain of sexual abuse, since road tests often become "sleeper tests." "You get 20 miles out of town, and the guy tells you to put out or get out." Gomez also contends that many firms use women truckers as "sexual rewards" by placing them with male drivers having good performance records.[108]

In *False Promises*, author Stanley Aronowitz quotes a worker from the Lordstown General Motors plant as saying, "Most men out there are perverted, dirty old men ... The foremen can be real nasty." Aronowitz reports that a worker became frustrated and left the job because of nervous tension resulting from inability to complain about problems on the job. When she did complain, the foremen would say, "If you can't do the work we'll get a man to do it.[109]

Ethnomethodological studies about on-the-job sex-role relationships could be conducted in varying work situations. In addition to examining the effect of sex-role attitudes on work-related behavior, the studies could investigate the impact of status differentiation between worker and boss, the type of work, as well as geographical and ethnic-cultural factors. Although these studies would be sociologically interesting and help a limited number of female workers and male bosses gain a better understanding of their interactions, they are probably less likely to lead directly toward policy change than the study mentioned above.[110]

HEALTH RIGHTS

How work affects people's health in other than the most obvious ways—black lung, loss of life, loss of limb—is only beginning to be explored by private researchers. It has yet to be addressed by U.S. government research conducted under the Occupational Safety and Health Act. Many work-related health problems affect both men and women, but the relationship between work and health does differ for women during pregnancy. In examining women's health issues, the Department of Labor and the Public Health Service have reported that despite pregnancies and contrary to popular myth, women workers have more favorable attendance records than men employed at similar job levels and under similar circumstances.[111]

Working Conditions and Women's Health

In June 1976, the Society for Occupational and Environmental Health (SOEH) held a conference on "Women and the Workplace." It focused on the causes of cancer, stillbirths, and birth defects and highlighted recently discovered health hazards such as anesthetic gases, ozone, and vinyl chloride as well as traditionally recognized hazards such as lead and infectious diseases. Chaired by Eula Bingham of the University of Cincinnati School of Medicine and Clara Schiffer of the Department of Health, Education, and Welfare (DHEW), the conference included participants from government, industry, labor, academia, and public interest groups. They discussed health risks associated with industries employing large numbers of women, legal issues raised by job placement patterns, regulatory problems, and society's responsibility for providing safe workplaces for women as well as for men.[112]

The conference and other discussions concerning workers' health and safety most poignantly highlight the conflict between the capitalistic profit motive and human beings' most basic needs. In 1970, over 14,000 workers died and 2.2 million were permanently or temporarily disabled on the job, according to DHEW statistics. Nearly a half-million additional workers developed officially recognized occupational diseases.[113] These statistics not only vastly underestimated the real numbers involved, but totally omitted officially unrecognized occupational diseases such as brown lung (byssinosis), which affects about 17,000 cotton, flax, and hemp workers (black lung was not officially recognized until 1969). In 1968, William H. Stewart, formerly surgeon general of the United States, stated that Public Health Service studies showed that 65 percent of American industrial workers were exposed to toxic materials or harmful physical conditions such as excessive noise or vibrations. Irving Selikoff, of the Mount Sinai Hospital in New York City, estimates that out of approximately 500,000 laborers now or previously working with asbestos, 100,000 will die of lung cancer and 35,000 of asbestosis (scarring of the lungs). In addition to the many men and women who must continue to work with substances that are known to be injurious to their health, many others are exposed to thousands of new chemicals that are annually introduced into industry without adequate testing or standards.[114]

Today over 20,000 chemicals are commonly found in most workplaces. Because chemicals are carried through air ducts in plants, they can affect pregnant women working where chemical substances are used or processed. Lead, vinyl chloride, chlorinated hydrocarbons, pesticides, solvents, anesthetic gases, ionizing radiation, methyl mercury, and other substances affect workers' reproductive systems by causing cancer, birth defects, central nervous system disorders, and other abnormalities in their offspring. Although 60 percent of American women work during their first pregnancies, few of the thousands of other chemicals commonly used have been tested for effects on the fetus.[115]

Nonchemical job characteristics also affect the health of both women and their offspring. Myra Wolfgang, former international vice president of the Hotel and Restaurant Employees Union, observed that although banquet waitressing is the "cream" of hotel-restaurant work, the pregnant waitress must carry forty-eight-pound trays and, like laundry workers and others who repeatedly lift heavy loads, she runs a high risk of aborting.[116] Similarly, health care facilities should be investigated to study how exposure to broken test tubes containing germs and to microwave ovens affects both fetuses and workers.[117] If these working conditions are found to endanger either workers or fetuses, extended paid maternity leaves and other policies should be instituted.

Research and policymaking should also focus on accumulated illnesses induced by long-term work on a particular job. The interests of men and women are joint rather than conflicting because both sexes have been exploited in this area. Epidemiologist Vilma Hunt has observed that exposures to noise, radiation, organic solvents, heat, toxic metals, and so forth are continually examined in terms of their economic impact on the industry concerned. In monitoring standarized mortality and morbidity rates for women workers, however, more data are needed to establish the relationship between occupational health and physiological characteristics.[118] Hemorrhoids and back trouble may develop from assembly line and other work; deafness from noisy machine rooms; foot problems from years of standing in laundry, dietary, and cafeteria jobs; high blood pressure, ulcers, strokes, and other tension-induced illnesses from exposure to noise, temperature extremes, rotating shift work, and lack of autonomy (e.g., being constantly watched, being pressured on the job); and lung and eye dysfunctions from steel and iron mill work. All of these and many other health-related work problems clearly need to be studied.

Attention must also be given to job-related health problems that occur more quickly. In using machines built according to a man's dimensions, for example, many women experience muscle strain or fatigue. Improper kitchen ventilation resulting in breathing difficulties as well as grease burns is a hazard of the restaurant industry. Polyethylene poisoning occurs in the meat-wrapping industry, and allergies are induced by fumes of permanent-press work in the textile industry. New studies to determine the relationships of tension, fatigue, health, safety, and the length of the workday in various types of jobs are needed to replace old studies that were conducted under obsolete conditions.[119] Such a study has been conducted by Rachelle Warren, of the University of Michigan, who found that "while women, in general, report twice as much stress as men, unemployed women report almost four times more stress in terms of mental and physcial health than unemployed men."[120]

Detailed questions related to weight lifting also deserve attention. What do men do if they are asked to lift more than they should? How can these solutions be adopted by women? What physical tests can be given to individual men and women to determine what jobs they can perform that will not damage their health? Furthermore, a summary, comparison, and evaluation of state and federal laws pertaining to weight lifting as well as other safety laws and their implementation is needed. How are employers informed of safety laws? How can enforcement of safety laws be improved? Employers should be required to design jobs that meet safety standards set by the National Institute of Occupational Safety and Health (NIOSH), which, in turn, must decide whether those standards have been met (e.g., will a job be too difficult for 80, 50, or 30 percent of all adults?).[121]

Government's, Industry's, and Workers'
Perspectives on Women's Health

The 1970 Occupational Safety and Health Act guarantees all workers the right to a safe and healthful workplace. Since 1970, however, workers may have actually experienced worsening job conditions. every year more chemicals are added to the workplace, and implementation of the act by the administering agencies, the Occupational Safety and Health Administration (OSHA) and NIOSH, has been severly hampered by business and probusiness adminstrators. During President Richard M. Nixon's first term, the newly formed OSHA was decentralized and splintered. President Gerald R. Ford repeatedly attacked OSHA in his 1976 government deregulation campaign. The Executive order requiring all federal agencies to prepare inflationary impact statements for new government standards has added many months to OSHA's twenty-two-step process for developing health and safety criteria. As of this writing, only three standards have been adopted. In addition, the agencies are under-funded, understaffed, and ineptly administered, according to a report by the Senate Committee on Labor and Public Welfare. There are not enough data on most potentially toxic chemicals for decisions to be made on the need for standards. In most cases where data indicate that chemicals are harmful, standards have not been developed; in the few cases where government standards have been developed, they have generally not been implemented. In 1974, OSHA appointed 800 inspectors to the 4.2 million workplaces in the United States—a discouraging proportion indeed.[122]

During the early and mid-1970s, women feared that discoveries concerning the impact of working conditions on fetuses and the development of protections for pregnant women would lead to renewed employer discrimination against women. Despite Title VII of the Civil Rights Act of 1964, which prohibits sex discrimination in hiring, promotion, layoff, and discharge policies of employers, several industries have "protected" women by barring them from employment. According to *The Spokeswoman:*

> The Lead Industries Association recently recommended that no nursing, pregnant, or fertile women be employed by the industry until more data on the reproductive effects of lead is available. Exxon Corporation is undertaking a study of the effects of benzene on women and will probably recommend that no women of childbearing age be exposed to that substance until the facts are in. The director of corporate medicine for Dow Chemical Corporation told the SOEH conference that his company has decided not to hire any women for jobs where they might be exposed to known human teratogens (substances which cause abnormalities in offspring) and transplacental carcinogens (substances which initiate cancer in fetuses exposed in the uterus). A similar response ... has also come from the [U.S.] Nuclear Regulatory Commission (NRC)—the only federal agency thus far to consider effects of work hazards on the fetus. The NRC considered mandatory pregnancy testing for workers and setting a separate radiation exposure for fertile women. The first of these alternatives was deemed an invasion of privacy and the second illegal sex discrimination. NRC also considered establishing a standard for all workers which would reduce the exposure limits to a tolerable level for even the fetus. This course was dropped because "reduction of the dose limits for all workers in order to avoid discrimination against women does not appear practicable. Such a reduction in the dose limits would cost the nuclear industry large sums of money...." So, the NRC instead developed "instructional guidelines" for pregnant workers which suggest, for example, that women "delay having children" until they can work in low exposure jobs or seek reassignment to low exposure jobs when they do become pregnant. If the latter is not possible, say the guidelines, "you might consider leaving your job."[123]

Workers, feminists, and unions have argued against these industrial actions. They maintain that the United States has established equal employment opportunity as a right regardless of sex and that being female for most women entails pregnancy. This fact was clearly recognized by Congress when it debated and passed Title VII of the

Civil Rights Act, the guidelines of which state, "A written or unwritten employment policy or practice which excludes from employment, applicants or employees because of pregnancy is in prima facie violation of Title VII of the Civil Rights Act."[124] The EEOC recently supported this position; however, to date, many state agencies or the government have not attempted to resolve the conflicts involved.[125]

Workers and feminists also observe that the United States is the only modern industrial nation that does not provide paid maternity leave.[126] In addition, in Sweden and the U.S.S.R., pregnant women are automatically transferred without loss of seniority or salary to plant areas where they are not exposed to toxic chemicals. (For a further discussion of maternity leave and benefits, see chapt. 5.) However, job transfer policies may fail to protect the fetus. Fetal injury may occur even before the worker knows she is pregnant. Also, recent research on men has shown that radiation, chemicals, and other work-related substances can damage offspring by affecting the sperm.[127]

Improved health standards for workers of both sexes would not only avoid possible discrimination against women by employers, but also provide the protection that adult men and women deserve. Until all chemical substances have been tested for their long- and short-term effects on adult population, a safe working hypothesis is that if substances cause damage to a fetus, then an adult may also be injured.

What can persons concerned with the health of workers do today? Since 88 percent of all women workers are unorganized, unionization is one answer. Most increases in health care services have come from the collective efforts of unionists who share work-related health and safety risks.[128] Members of the CLUW and other unionized workers can collect statistics and other information on their own health experiences as well as pressure companies and the government to conduct research and enforce standards.

There must be systematic epidemiological studies by sociologists, medical doctors, and chemists on the effects of all chemical, nuclear, and other work-related substances on workers and fetuses. Health hazards of jobs that employ large numbers of women should be studied first, but the hazards of traditionally male jobs now being entered by women must not be ignored.

American researchers who decide to study the health questions raised above should first review the research literature of other nations to determine precisely what medical questions need to be answered or made known to the American public and policymakers. West Germany, for example, which has several institutes in industrial medicine, is far ahead of the United States in research on industrial health.[129]

The cost of the studies and enforcement of health standards is not a valid issue. The United States cannot afford the much larger costs of millions of children born with birth defects because of its ignorance of job hazards.

HOURS OF WORK

Historically, the length of the workday has been a major rallying issue for workers. Today, both the number of hours that are worked per week and how these hours are scheduled are matters of concern. State protective laws, intended to protect women against long working hours, have been repealed.[130] Many blue-collar women as well as men must work ten-hour days and six-day weeks.

The six-day workweek means that workers must do their shopping, laundry, and other housework on the seventh day, with no day for rest. This schedule has negative effects on the morale, physical and mental health, and family life of both male and female workers. The long hours and their effects on workers should be documented, widely publicized, and changed. Toward this end, the Department of Labor could routinely publish in its *Employment and Earnings* the numbers of hours that women and men work weekly.

More complex is the question of how to make work schedules maximally compatible with family life. Furthermore, how do various work schedules affect blue-collar women and their families? At a time when the ten-hour day, four-day week is being considered, the effect of differing types of work schedules on various groups of women and their families (single, married but childless, married with children, and single with children) should be examined carefully. To date, although the four-day week has been widely debated, its potential impact on working women and their families has been largely unexamined.[131] Many companies and governmental units have already shifted to the four-day, ten-hour week. The positive and negative effects of these schedules on the women and their family lives could be determined through interviews. In these studies, researchers should examine whether some women have intentionally avoided jobs under the new schedules and, if so, why.

Similarly, the impact on workers and their families of existing combinations of night and day shifts seven days a week, offer the following monthly schedule: afternoons, 4-12 P.M., off fifty-six hours;

days, 8 A.M.-4 P.M., off thirty hours; nights, 12 P.M.-8 A.M. for seven days, off ninety-six hours (four days). Some workers have a steady workday with either afternoon or night shift throughout the year.

A related issue concerns how plants administer overtime policies. How often is the manner in which overtime is to be distributed spelled out in job contracts? How do these agreements affect women and their families? How is overtime distributed when the process is not specified in job contracts? At a minimum, all overtime over forty hours per week or eight hours per day must be voluntary and paid at the rate of time-and-a-half for all men and women. As a first step, all unions could set up their own system of voluntary overtime, as some already have done. In the system of working "down the list," for example, a member is offered the opporutnity to work overtime. If she or he does not want to do so, the union proceeds down the list.[132]

For overtime to be truly voluntary, workers must be paid wages for a forty-hour week that are adequate to support a family. The Bureau of Labor Statistics (BLS) standard for an intermediate family income budget described above could be used as the criterion for minimum wages. For an urban family of four, this standard was $15,318 in autumn 1975.[133] The 1974 mean per capita, before-tax income in the United States was $5,449. For a family of four, this income increased to $21,796. In other words, if income were distributed equally or nearly equally, no family would fall below the BLS standard. Furthermore, the incomes of over 80 percent of American families which now fall below the mean would be increased.[134]

Flexible hours are also a critical factor for blue-collar employed mothers. Enjoyed normally by professional workers, time off from work is needed, for example, to allow blue-collar women to take themselves or their children to the dentist or doctor, shop for clothes, or visit a school play. Time-budget studies, organized according to industry and occupation, should be conducted to determine the hours that women spend working, commuting, and doing domestic work in order to acquaint the public and legislature with the women's plight.[135] Special attention should be devoted to the hours worked on the job, the transportation difficulties in commuting that could be ameliorated, and features of American living patterns that could be improved to reduce domestic working hours: communal washers and dryers used by four to six families, which would free women from driving to and remaining at a laundromat; play area to reduce the time parents spend watching over their own children; and social policies to encourage fathers to share housework and childcare.[136]

Part-time work as well as a shorter workweek could also answer the needs of many mothers with young children. From 1963 to 1973, part-time employment of adult women grew by 54 percent, compared with a 28 percent increase in full-time employment. In 1979, of the 43 million adult women in the civilian force, 11.9 million were either working or seeking to work part time.[137] The kinds of benefits available to part-time employees in major companies of various industries should be investigated. There should be studies on union and employer attitudes about part-time work rewarded by pay and benefits proportionate to the time worked, followed by experimental demonstation research projects that focus on the problems raised. Industry-by-industry cost and productivity studies, including records of absenteeism of part-time workers, should be made. Anne Nelson, associate director of the Trade Union Women's Studies Program at Cornell University, has pointed out that some unions have managed to integrate part-time workers into their union activities and thus extended union benefits to them. How do these unions accomplish this task? Are there peculiar conditions? Can other unions learn from these experiences?[138] Legislation concerning the part-time workers' rights— their wages, benefits, and security of employement—is needed.

In addition, part-time work at adequate wages for fathers as well as mothers of young children might be accepted by blue-collar families.[139] Since workers may prefer a shorter workweek, surveys should be conducted to determine how many would support a thirty-five or thirty-hour workweek. To be workable, all research and social policies related to working hours must recognize that the vast majority of working women bear and raise children sometime during their lives.

JOB BENEFITS

Benefits are often distributed more unequally than wages among workers and managers. For example, sociologist Robert Schrank has pointed out that, unlike white-collar workers, blue-collar workers lack telephones for personal use. Free access to telephones is important to all workers, particularly parents, since a telephone call after school will allow children to feel close to their working parents and allow the parents to discuss with the children how they will spend the remainder of their afternoon. Free access to telephones is even more important when a child is ill. In addition, a call to a friend may break the monotony of the day or the alienation of the workplace and result in better mental health among workers.

Similarly, released time to visit a dentist or doctor is taken for granted and not even requested by most managerial and professional workers. It is a consideration that would help ease the lives of blue-collar workers.

Fringe benefits such as pension insurance rights are discussed in chapter 5 under "Company, Government, and Union Benefits." A major national survey should be conducted on fringe benefits accrued to women from industry to industry, job to job, and union to union. The findings of this study and the importance of fringe benefits should be made known to women looking for jobs.

HISTORICAL, DEMOGRAPHIC, AND ETHNOGRAPHIC RESEARCH ON WORKING CONDITIONS

Historical research must be conducted to understand present social policies and working conditions. Furthermore, trend analyses could be used to account for historical shifts in women's wages as well as the percentage of women working in various blue-collar, industrial, and service jobs. To what extent are women's wages, training opportunities, and job opportunities correlated with national economic conditions such as recession, government spending, and foreign competition as well as historical events such as wars? What can be done in the future to prevent these events from disproportionately affecting women?

Demographic studies as well as census data must be used in guiding policymakers and pressure groups. With the aid of county or city census information on women's wages by occupation and ethnicity, local politicians and others should be adequately informed of the status of women in their communities. On the national level, census data should be gathered in an effort to construct pictures of working and living conditions of various groups of employed blue-collar women and to better understand the types of social policies that are required to help these groups. In addition, census data can provide a better understanding of pay differentials in industries. William H. Chafe pointed out that in 1951, wherever females constituted more than 50 percent of an industry's labor force, the industry paid a wage below the national average.[140] Elsewhere, Barry Bluestone has shown that Department of Defense subsidization of particular industries significantly raised the wage levels of those industries when factors of unionization, geographic location, and occupation were held constant.[141] To understand the extent to which these factors operate today, census data should be considered along with participant-observer workplace studies to learn the degree of double discrimination against white ethnic, black, chicano, Puerto Rican, Filipino, and Chinese women.[142] Finally, census data can be used to determine how many full-time "working poor" persons are working women with children.

To understand the needs of women, policymakers and social change agents will also need ethnographic, descriptive studies on working-class women's occupations and lives. Studies must address wages, on-the-job training opportunities, and promotion opportunities for paraprofessionals and aides in education, legal work, police duty, and nursing. In addition, indepth interviews should be conducted with paraprofessional and other blue-collar, industrial and service workers. Interviews could include questions on how they view their jobs (i.e., how do they see their morning, their afternoon?) and how they believe their jobs can be improved for themselves and their families. Finally, policymakers should be enlightened by summary studies of the status of and policies affecting blue-collar employed women in other nations.

CHAPTER 4. WORK, TRAINING,
PROMOTION OPPORTUNITIES

THE RIGHT TO WORK

Presently, many blue-collar women worry more about obtaining work than about their working conditions. In 1979, according to the Bureau of Labor Statistics, the unemployment rate for women was 6.8 percent as compared with 5.1 percent for men.[143] Women aged 16-19 years had an unemployment rate of 16.4 percent, and minority women of this age cohort had an unemployment rate of 35.7 percent.[144] The number of unemployed married women nearly doubled over the year ending March 1975; their unemployment rate reached 8.5 percent as compared with 6.1 percent for married men—the highest rate recorded since 1940. About half of the unemployed married women reported job loss as the reason for unemployment, up sharply from March 1974, but a clear departure from the usual pattern where entry or reentry is the major reason.[145] Overall, the number of unemployed women has increased greatly, and women account for an increasing proportion of all unemployed persons. In 1977, over 3.2 million women were unemployed and accounted for 48 percent of all unemployed persons as compared with 32 percent in 1950.[146]

Despite the severity of these statistics, they omit many unemployed women. Bertram Gross has "conservatively estimated" that 5 million housewives desire work and would work if suitable employment were available;[147] however, none of the 5 million were counted in the Department of Labor's statistics on the unemployed. Government unemployment statistics including procedures for counting and reporting the unemployed should therefore be reexamined and restructured. Women currently not included in statistics on unemployment are those who desire or need work but are unable to work because of inadequate childcare; those who work ten, twenty, or thirty hours a week but desire or need work on a full-time schedule; those unemployed for ten or eleven months of the year but employed only during the month of the employment count; and those who would like to work but have looked for a job for so long that they gave up the search over the last four weeks.[148]

Marilyn Bender and Seymour Wolfbein, for example, closely watch labor force statistics and warn of a backlash developing against affirmative action because of the recession, which threatens the expanding role of women as workers in America.[149] As jobs become scarcer, an increasing number of women are afraid to continue raising affirmative action issues and legitimate grievances for fear of losing their jobs. For this reason, Gloria Johnson has pointed out the need to study the effect of economic conditions on the number of complaints about sex discrimination and explore procedural means of protecting women from discrimination during recessionary times.[150]

The recession has also led to serious court battles over the principle of seniority versus the principle of affirmative action.[151] This has led to differences among women's organizations. The National Organization for Women (NOW) charged that the seniority system discriminates against women workers. Olga Madar, past president of the Coalition of Labor Union Women (CLUW), countered by stating that "more women are losing jobs in unorganized workplaces that do not have the protection of seniority than the number of women being laid off from organized workplaces who do have the protection of seniority."[152] In a meeting of summer 1975, the National Coordinating Committee of the CLUW resolved to "explore ways to promote full employment, ... declared that the costs of past discrimination are the employer's responsibility and that governmental and tax support should prevent layoffs and closures," and urged its members "to seek to improve the seniority system in their union contracts to eliminate aspects that have not served women and minority groups fairly."[153]

Included among the issues of employment opportunities and unemployment statistics is the right to work. For men and women of different races, creeds, and nationalities, the right to work guarantees a major advancement beyond the right to equal opportunity to compete for work.

The Murray-Wagner Full Employment Bill of 1945 had guaranteed regular, useful, and remunerative employment for all Americans who were able and willing to work. If the bill were passed and implemented today, then the problems resulting from forced unemployment—poverty, unhappiness, and, in some cases, mental illness—would be eliminated, thus creating a more productive and richer nation.

The basic principles of the Murray-Wagner bill were revived early in the 94th Congress by Representative Augustus Hawkins, who concluded from a study of his own district of Watts that affirmative action laws were of limited use in a depressed job market. Hawkins introduced the bill as the Equal Opportunity and Full Employment Act. It was retitled the Balanced Growth and Full Employment Act, introduced by the late Senator Hubert H. Humphrey in the Senate, and redrafted. After "equal opportunity" was struck from its title, representatives of women's groups, Congressman Hawkins, Congresswoman Burke, and others drafted language to meet the needs of women by the addition of equal pay clauses and the requirement that "every effort" be made toward "the ultimate goal of removing" employment differentials "entirely." The Humphrey-Hawkins bill died in 1976 with the adjournment of the 94th Congress. (Prior to this writing, however, President Carter endorsed a compromise version of the Humphrey-Hawkins bill.)[154]

Full employment and equal opportunity nevertheless continue to be issues and must remain so until full employment is a reality for all groups.[155] The AFL-CIO, for example, recommended to Congress that the Federal Reserve Board justify to the president and Congress the manner in which its monetary policies will help meet full employment targets.[156]

The right to work should include the right to work part-time for those who wish it, the right to train for work, and the right to assistance in finding a job. Changing rapidly the attitudes and procedures of state and private employment officers across the nation will encourage rather than prevent women from applying for the higher-paying traditionally male jobs. This action research should be conducted on a nationwide basis until all employment offices stop maintaining separate job files for men and women or in any way discourage women from applying for traditionally male positions. Changes are also called for on the part of the employers and armed services recruiters. Research is no longer needed to document the sexist attitudes of both; rather, a concerted effort accompanied by evaluation research is needed that will spread information concerning affirmative action laws among employers, recruiters, and women job applicants; inform employers that beliefs such as women having higher absenteeism than men are incorrect; and induce employers and armed services recruiters to seek women for traditionally male jobs as well as help them learn and adjust to the jobs.

Some employment office procedures such as separate job files for men and women deprive women of the right to work in a straightforward way, while other procedures are more subtle. It is not known, for example, how mechanical tests discriminate against women, or how many employers ask women whether they plan to have children and then bar from work those who honestly answer yes. Nor is it known how many employers try to force women to retire at age sixty-two through social security laws. Although we know that outright discrimination and English language requirements bar many ethnic and Third World women from work, we do not know the extent to which American lack of knowledge about and empathy with their cultures keeps these women from obtaining or keeping jobs. For example, Chela Sandoval has pointed out that Chicanas are taught to be more quiet and less assertive than American women. They are also taught to lower their eyes rather than look directly at persons to whom they are to show respect, including those who are older, more educated, or hold a higher position than themselves.[157] Research on how American ethnocentrism concerning these and other cultural traits results in discimination against white ethnic, Chicano, Native American, Puerto Rican, oriental, and black women should be conducted and followed by remedial action accompanied by evaluation research.

Unemployment data and other research show that minority women aged 16-19, women with large numbers of children, and older women who have been out of the labor force for a considerable length of time in order to raise children have the greatest difficulty in obtaining work. Experimental research on job subsidies, training programs similar to those for veterans, and other inducements should be conducted to determine by what means employees might be most effectively encouraged to hire, retain, and promote these women. Furthermore, Alexis Herman, former director of the Black Women's Employment Program and current director of the U.S. Women's Bureau, has noted, "It behooves us to take a systematic look at the traditional job referral offices that are supposed to service the employment needs of minority communities." In 1974, in Atlanta, Georgia, Herman's employment program placed "more minority women in decent paying jobs than the Georgia State Employment office had in the past *four* years."[158]

THE RIGHT TO TRAINING

In the United States, lack of training or education has been overemphasized as a cause of unemployment and poverty.[159] The extremely low unemployment rates during World War II meant that many people were "unemployable" because of lack of training and other factors in times of low labor force demand; however, they were indeed "employable" when the labor force demand was high enough. Nevertheless, individuals must have the right to train for work in which they are interested. In an ideal tomorrow, when jobs are no longer sharply differentiated by prestige and pay, training will allow individuals to have variety in their work by enabling them to move from job to job. Today, training represents a step toward a more interesting, more prestigious, or better-paying job.

Although federal laws forbid sex discrimination, blatant discrimination has been documented in both military and civilian government-sponsored education and training programs.[160] In federal training programs such as the Job Corps and Work Incentive Program (WIN), vocational education, public high schools, apprenticeship training, career education, and on-the-job training companies, women are still frequently informed about and trained for low-paying, traditionally female work such as secretarial and homemaking jobs. Furthermore, counselors and teachers associated with these programs often misinform women students by convincing those who are wives and mothers that they will not need to work, when in fact their husbands are unble to support a family alone. They neglect to discuss current divorce rates and the corresponding high probability that many women students as young adults will have to support themselves and their children. In addition, they do not inform students of the best job opportunities by occupational projections for the next thirty years.

Vocational Education

The Department of Labor sponsored the Wisconsin Women in Apprenticeship Project and observed that of 350 government-approved apprenticeable trades, Wisconsin women were involved in only 10.[161] It further reported:

> The entire apprenticeship establishment was composed almost exclusively of males, most of whom had themselves graduated

through the apprenticeship system—from the journeyman supervisor to the technical school classroom theory instructor. Even the apprenticeship representatives in state government, who registered apprenticeship training agreements, were generally recruited from the ranks of journeymen, the rationale being that they had experience, and therefore understood the apprenticeship system.[162]

The public school system was also found to have serious sex stereotyping and discrimination. According to the report:

> 98.5 percent of the enrollees in Wisconsin high school industrial classes were male. The girls are given home economics or, if they are not in the college track, business subjects. In most schools girls are either overtly forbidden or subtly discouraged from seriously experimenting with shop courses that lay the foundation for work in the skilled trades: too great an interest in, or proficiency at, things technical are considered "unfeminine." This puts most women at a disadvantage when taking selection tests that examine familiarity with the tools and terms of the trade.[163]

Government employees administering job training and placement programs were found equally at fault:

> Most had almost no understanding of the implications of the equal rights laws, were completely unfamiliar with the Equal Employment Opportunity Commission's narrow interpretation of sex as a *bona fide* occupational qualification, and had not heard of Order 4, which mandated affirmative action programs to remedy the effects of past discrimination on the part of governmet contractors. All the government-sponsored manpower training programs initially contracted by the Project exhibited rampant sex stereotyping. Job Corps, Jobs Options, Labor Education Advancement Program, Work Incentive Program—all suffered, as did the Employment Service itself, from the need to meet quantitative placement goals as cheaply and economically as possible. Broadening employer or client horizons for vocational choice takes additional staff time and energy and the system has awarded no extra credit for quality of placement—in skilled trade training as opposed to a dead-end job, for instance.[164]

Action projects accompanied by evaluation research should be undertaken throughout the country to bring vocational education, job training, and apprenticeship programs in line with the standards set by equal employment laws. Table 2 provides a picture of the distribution of women and men in the several areas of vocational education. Of the 6.4 million women and girls enrolled in public vocational programs in the United States in 1972 (the most recent date for which statistics are available), 50 percent were being trained in home economics and another 30 percent in office practices.[165] While little effort is being made to guide women into higher-paying, less female-stereotyped occupations, the National Planning Association estimates that by 1980, 20.1 million job openings will primarily occur in traditionally male occupations for which high schools offer vocational courses with entry-level preparation.[166]

Opening up tchnical vocational education to women may help women acquire high-paying skilled jobs.[167] One difficulty with this approach is that vocational education for men now has its own problems, including outdated training for available jobs, training for nonexistent jobs, and very traditional teachers.[168] Although male vocational school graduates are introducd to the use of various machines through a wide range of jobs in the schools, less than one quarter are actually placed in jobs through the schools.[169] More women than men, however, need these introductions. Although men obtain jobs more frequently through friends and relatives than through vocational schools, women are often barred from skilled jobs on the grounds that they lack vocational training.

Vocational education required two simultaneous actions. First, by adapting the curriculum and counseling to updated labor force projections, both men and women will benefit. This action should not only gear training programs to jobs for which there will be a demand for the next ten years, but also establish a full-credit course in which students are taught about labor force projections and the range of jobs with considerable demand in the future. The second needed action is to involve women on an equal basis with men in every stage of vocational education, from student recruitment to career counseling and training to followup on how they do on the job.

It is now known what proportion of women, given a real opportunity, would choose to move into traditionally male jobs. However, all the information suggests that, given a choice, women would move into every level of the industrial hierarchy.[170] Indeed, between 1960 and 1970, when some doors were opened to women, the rate of increase of women in the skilled trades was eight times the rate of increase for men.[171]   .

In 1974, $40 million was appropriated for vocational education research and development under the authority of the Vocational Education Amendments of 1968 (Public Law 90-576)[172] and administered by the Bureau of Occupational and Adult Education of the U.S. Office of Education. Additional sums were appropriated for vocational education research and development by the Department of Defense, the Department of Labor, the National Institute of Education, other federal agencies, the states independent of state-administered federal funds, and private foundations.

Little of this multimillion-dollar funding was devoted to projects directly related to the needs of women.[173] In 1974, only one out of the 93 federally funded projects under Section 131 (a), Part C of the Vocational Education Amendments of 1968 pertained directly to women.[174] The allocation of so few Part C funds to projects for women is all the more striking given the critical observation in the previous year by the National Advisory Council on Extension and Continuing Education that " ... although the legislative language [of Part C, Section 132 of the Vocational Education Act] is general enough to permit funding of demonstration projects relevant to the needs of mature women ... only one project has been funded with any relevance to the concerns of women."[175]

Furthermore, no projects for women were funded in 1974 under the federally administered Part I or the regionally administered Part D of the amendment.[176] Of the fifty state offices of vocational education in 1975, only three sponsored substantial research to determine how vocational education might better serve girls and women.[177] In the future, research and development projects should be funded and conducted to:

- Determine how to recruit women most effectively, which enables them to remain in a wide variety of vocational programs that are stereotypically male
- Determine means of assisting women most effectively in making the transition from vocational school to high-paying jobs that have traditionally employed few or no women
- Determine the characteristics, including the counseling and

educational preparation, of female students who are successful in various traditionally male and traditionally female vocational education programs

- Survey high school students, vocational education teachers, and counselors regarding their perceptions of future work patterns of female students
- Determine the availability of vocational education for pregnant teenagers
- Analyze the content of all vocational education texts as well as curricular and counseling materials for sex stereotypes and other forms of sexism.
- Develop nonsexist text books as well as other curricular and counseling materials for every area of vocational education
- Survey persons of both sexes in vocational education programs and jobs traditionally considered the prerogative of the other sex and learn what overt and covert barriers are to be confronted
- Determine what positive and negative sanctions occur at various stages of vocational guidance and counseling for persons to consider occupations traditionally considered the prerogative of the other sex.
- Study vocational educational counseling and instructional processes to determine exactly how counselors and teachers advise female as compared with male students and what aspects of the advising process most influence female students from various racial, ethnic, geographic, cultural, and economic backgrounds and of various ages and grade levels.
- Determine the effects of different forms of vocational counseling on female students with varying backgrounds, needs, and problems.
- Through a series of experimental demonstration research projects, find the best means by which counselors and teachers may help elementary, junior, and senior high school girls to consider a wide range of traditionally male as well as traditionally female job possibilities while helping them select courses that have long-range usefulness for evaluating the desirability of postsecondary education
- Determine the most effective means to overcome occupational sex stereotypes that dampen the motivations of girls in pursuit of traditionally male careers

- Determine how females of all ages from various racial, ethnic, geographic, cultural, and economic backgrounds make career decisions
- Develop measures of career development based on samples including adequate numbers of women and minorities of various backgounds as well as majority males and follow the samples through their later career development to determine the usefulness of the measures
- Determine means of encouraging and enabling more women to develop and submit proposals for research and development funds
- Determine the most effective means of teaching elementary school and vocational education students about the changing career patterns of women, the implications of manpower projections for students' occupational choices, and federal and state equal employment laws
- Determine the most effective means of educating parents, community, and business groups about the need to open traditionally male occupations to women
- Survey female vocational graduates in a variety of traditional and nontraditional jobs concerning means by which their vocational instruction and counseling might have been improved and how it benefited them
- Determine the most effective means of teaching female students to seek, apply, interview, and begin work in nontraditional jobs
- Determine the effectiveness of simulated work samples and problems from traditionally male jobs that familiarize female students with various types of work by allowing them to assess their interests and abilities

The U.S Commissioner of Education should provide for the dissemination of all research findings on means of improving the effectiveness of vocational education for women to all state vocational education directors, directors of state vocational education offices for women, and directors of vocational education systems within the United States.

Giving priority to the Women's Rights Project, the American Civil Liberties Union Foundation recently identified sex discrimination in vocational education to be a major problem. As part of this project, a number of lawsuits on behalf on individuals will be filed against particular schools that discriminate in vocational education. A lawsuit will then be filed against the Department of Health, Education, and Welfare for failing and refusing to enforce the law.[178]

In the spring of 1975, Congress began to examine carefully the needs of women in vocational education. The House Subcommittee on Elementary, Secondary, and Vocational Education held three days of hearings under the chairpersonships of Representatives Carl Perkins and Shirley Chisholm on sex discrimination and sex stereotyping in vocational educations.[179] The first of a series of bills on women's vocational education was proposed by Senator Walter Mondale in the following November.[180] The outcome of these efforts has been the inclusion of provisions concerning women in vocational education in the Education Act Amendments of 1976 (Public Law 94-482). *The Spokeswoman* has summarized the new provisions:

> To qualify for funds under the $1.09-billion federal vocational education program, a state is to assign full-time staff to monitor sex discrimination laws, submit recommendations for ending sex bias, make sure women's needs are addressed in state grants and generally reduce sex stereotyping in vocational education. States are required to spend $50,000 in this area, but may assign personnel only "as necessary." States must also draw up five-year plans stating goals for reducing sex bias and strategies for meeting goals before receiving federal grant money. Among the policies a state must adopt are those to insure equal vocational educational opportunities for men and women. Authorized uses of vocational education funds include support services for women entering nontraditional fields, day care services and training for displaced homemakers, single heads of household and part-time working homemakers who wish to work full-time. The law requires that women familiar with sex discrimination be included on state and national vocational advisory councils.... Unfortunately, no national group currently monitors programs for women in vocational education.[181]

Apprenticeship Programs

Apprenticeship programs must also be opened to women. In 1976, women constituted slightly over 1 percent of all 267,645 registered apprentices.[182] Programs such as the Wisconsin Women in Apprenticeship Project, successfully established in one locality, should now be implemented in every city of the nation. During the mid-1970s, the Department of Labor has devoted considerable publicity to gains women have made through its apprenticeship program, WIN, the Comprehensive Employment Training Act (CETA), and on-the-job training programs.[183] This publicity has been useful because it has increased the acceptability of women entering higher-paid, traditionally male jobs; however, the progress made should not be overemphasized. *Women Today* has questioned what constitutes "making headway" in apprenticeship participation after observing that the march 1976 *ETA Interchange*, published by the Employment and Training Administration of the Department of Labor, reported, "'Women represented another group making headway in apprenticeship participation. There were an estimated 400 women in training in 1964. There were 3,700 in training in 1974, an eightfold increase, bringing women to 1 percent of the total number of apprentices in 1974.' The next paragraph indicated that the number of veterans participating in apprenticeship programs had climbed from an estimated 78,000 in 1964 to more than 130,700 in 1974—a 67 percent increase."[184] By measuring women's position within apprenticeship programs, it is obvious that more progress should be made for women to obtain equality in the programs.

Apprenticeship programs for women must be operated over a considerable period of time because eradicating barriers to women in apprenticeship requires several separate sequential actions. To increase the number of women in apprenticeships and to expand the range of occupations for which women might apply and be accepted for apprenticeships, the Wisconsin project had to (1) change the attitudes and practices of employers and unions; (2) motivate women; and (3) change the attitudes and procedures of those in government agencies, the educational system, and the legal regulatory system.[185] Because most blue-collar women do not realize until their late 20s or early 30s that they will have to work most of their lives, elimination of young age limits (usually twenty-six years) for apprenticeship programs was an important procedural change initiated by the project.

Eradicating sex discrimination in existing apprenticeship programs will be difficult. Its impact will also be limited by the small fraction of skilled, apprenticeable jobs and the high competition for positions in these jobs.[186] There is an oversupply of labor in these high-paying skilled trades because the nation did not undertake the construction of homes, rapid transit systems, schools, parks, and other badly needed facilities. Should the nation seriously attempt to meet its needs in these areas, there would be a shortage of personnel in the skilled trades. Nonetheless, even given today's practices, one may argue on ethical grounds that opening up apprenticeship training to women is important, since by apprenticeship a person may be paid to learn a skilled trade that will eventually command a wage sufficient to maintain a family at a level well above poverty. Opening apprenticeships may also have a "trickle down" effect, leading employers and unions to accept women in less prestigious skilled and unskilled jobs requiring little or no training.

Norma Briggs, coordinator of the Wisconsin Women in Apprenticeship Project, and others have also argued that demonstration research and action are needed to create apprenticeships in occupations that currently have none.[187] For example, cutters in the sewing division of automobile companies are taught informally on the job. In such situations, white men often maintain their positions by assuring that only friends and relatives will be hired and by teaching the jobs only to friends and relatives of lower seniority. Formal on-the-job training sponsored by the company or the union could eliminate nepotism, which bars women and minorities from high-paying, relatively easy occupations. Companies or unions should insist that placement and training of women and minorities in all jobs be part of the job descriptions for managers and stewards and that performance in this aspect of their jobs will be assessed, rewarded, or punished as is performance of their other duties. In large plants, special managers could be hired to guarantee that women and minorities receive equitable, informal on-the-job training.

Still others have suggested that traditionally female or nonprofessional jobs such as childcare attendants, pratical nurses, and homemakers be made apprenticeable so that recognized standards for formal on-the-job training may be established.[188] In addition, Nancy Seifer, who has worked extensively with women in working-class neighborhoods, recommends midcareer grants for women workers, which would provide for continuing education or training for women in new and expanding fields.[189] She notes that after childrearing many women are ready and have the right to make entirely new career decisions. For such continuing education for women to be successful, Joyce Kornbluh, of the University of Michigan Institute for Industrial and Labor Relations, has observed that special services must be provided.

More weekend courses and centers of continuing education for women blue-collar workers would include lounges and libraries as well as tutorial help, scholariships, counseling, training for job interviews, childcare, brown-bag lunches, and library instruction, thus making community colleges and universities more attractive and useful. Research should be conducted at several colleges to discover additional ways of assisting blue-collar women, and existing university degree programs for workers should be monitored for problems involving sexism.

During the New York City Trade Union Women's Program, Barbara Wertheimer and Anne Nelson of Cornell University discovered that working women had a high degree of commitment to higher education. The women's ages ranged from twenty to sixty years; two-thirds were black or Hispanic, all the women were employed, and many were heads of families and committed to union responsibilites as well. When Wertheimer and Nelson asked the women, "How do you manage all that you do?," they discovered that what the women had given up was sleep, averaging only 4½ to 6 hours a night.[190]

Retraining programs in England, West Germany, and France, which provide excellent models for the United States, offer anyone a one-year training stipend at nearly full salary.[191] In Vienna, Austria, orientation programs also exist for women who want to return to work. These week-long orientation programs encourage women in their 40s and 50s to attend. The mornings provide programs that offer informational lectures about social security, training programs, and budgetary matters, and the afternoons include visits to factories, offices, and hospitals where women are able to talk with the personnel manager about what to expect when returning to work. The women who choose to return to work by the end of the orientation week are given dates for counseling with the labor office and, if necessary, are advised about training programs. In Australia, on the other hand, companies are so desperate for labor that they are seeking women to work for them by going door to door.[192]

Currently, the Job Corps trains hundreds of women for secretarial jobs but pays wages lower than the women need to support their households; WIN, the federal employment and training program with the largest number of women, places women who are heads of households in jobs paying poverty-level wages. The Job Corps, WIN, and other federal training programs should hire trainers, counselors, and placement officers to change employer and client attitudes about appropriate jobs for women. Researchers and affirmative action coordinators should be hired in each region to monitor and find new ways of facilitating affirmative action placement of women in traditionally male jobs.

To be totally successful, affirmative action programs must begin with blue-collar daughters at an early eage—in kindergarten, grade school, and organizations for girls (e.g., the Girl Scouts). Stories told to these girls should reflect women's movement into traditionally male positions. Girls as well as boys should be encouraged to exercise not only for their general health but also so that they will develop stength to qualify for various jobs. For their mothers, the federal government should develop special advertising, placement services, and preference for veterans of motherhood as it has for veterans of foreign wars.

PROMOTION OPPORTUNITIES

Many factors other than training affect the promotion of women. Basic research is needed to understand the practices of employers in promoting women. An industry-by-industry study should be made of the promotion patterns of women as compared with men. The study should include personal characteristics (e.g., age, race, education), geographical location, industry, and union.

The impact of different forms of job posting on women and minorities should also be investigated. What forms of job posting are most effective in various types of work situations? A related promotional research issue that should be undertaken is a sweeping investigation of how various companies treat maternity leave in contract seniority provisions. The federal and state governments should develop a system of rewards to encourage industry to promote women, and industry in turn should create a system to encourage its management to promote women.

CHAPTER 5. LIVING CONDITIONS

The off-the-job living conditions of blue-collar employed women are affected by a number of factors: wages; company, union, and government benefits; community services; and actions and attitudes of husbands and family members. This section examines research and policy needs to improve living conditons.

WAGES

Over the last decade, rising inflation has eaten away at the ability of the working class to improve or even maintain its standard of living.[193] As a result, many blue-collar women have been pushed into the labor force and, in many cases, deprived of their hope to own a home.

For the purposes of organization and political action, actual trends in the purchasing power of blue-collar employed women by industry, occupation, and geographical area of residence should be investigated. What can the blue-collar woman buy with her wages? To what extent can the financial needs of the single mother, the single woman, and the wife be met by these wages? There must also be a better understanding of how these women are affected by certain factors—education, discrimination, and the crowding of women into sex-segregated work (see chapt. 3). Barry Bluestone and Mary Stevenson have found other wage determinants. They have noted that the American economy is a tripartite organization. The three segments, the "core economy," the "peripheral economy," and the "irregular economy," have unique industrial characteristics and individual labor markets:

> The core economy includes those industries which comprise the muscle of American economic and political power. [It] is by far the largest sector of the three in terms of financial resources.

Entrenched in durable manufacturing, the construction trades, and to a lesser extent, the extraction industries, the firms in the core economy are noted for high productivity, high profits, intensive utilization of capital, high incidence of monopoly elements, and a high degree of unionization. The automobile, steel, rubber, aluminum, aerospace, and petroleum industries are ranking members of that part of the economy. Workers who are able to secure employment in these industries are, in most cases, assured of relatively high wages and better than average working conditions and fringe benefits.

The peripheral economy: Beyond the fringes of the core economy lies a set of industries which lack almost all of the advantages normally found in center firms. Concentrated in subprofessional services, retail trade, agriculture and nondurable manufacturing, the peripheral industries are noted for their small firm size, labor intensity, low profits, low productivity, intensive product competition, lack of unionization, and consequently low wages. Unlike core sector industries the periphery lacks the assets, the sheer size, and the political power to take advantages of economies of scale or spend large sums on reserch and development. At the present rate, the peripheral industries are more than likely doomed to a continuation of the "repressive economic environment" they are accustomed to. The workers who are trapped in the periphery become the working poor.

The irregular economy includes the vast bulk of monetized economic activity which is not included in the national income accounts. The "industries" in this sector, mainly concentrated in the ghetto, have escaped the scrutiny of the Social Security Administration and the Internal Revenue Service by remaining informal and only loosely attached to the organized network of the regular economy. To a great extent, the irregular economy involves:

1. informal work patterns that are frequently invisible to outside observers;
2. an organized set of occupational roles specific to ghetto life;
3. work skills and competencies that are a product of ghetto life; and

4. the acquisition of work skills and competencies through nontraditional channels.

Some of the work opportunities in the irregular economy are deviant by middle class moral and legal standards (prostitution and dope peddling), but most are not. Job activities may range from daily contract work for gardening to plumbing, electrical work, and automobile repair. These job experiences allow the worker to engage in pseudoentrepreneurial activity that is closed to him in the other two sectors of the economy.[194]

The U.S. government affects the wages of all workers and the differential wage rates of the core and peripheral economies in important ways. Through billions of dollars of federal purchases, the well-paid workers in the core economy become richer with tax dollars paid by everyone, including the poorer peripheral-economy workers. As characteristics of education, occupation, geographical location, and sex are constant, persons earn significantly less in the peripheral than in the core economy. For example, in Detroit female janitors with ten years of education average lower earnings in retail shops than in automobile plants. Women are most heavily concentrated in the lower paying peripheral and men in the higher paying core economy.[195]

Bluestone has specified the impact placed on wages by all levels of government:

Federal, state, and local governments combined are responsible for nearly a third of the annual output of the whole economy, and the distribution of government purchases is heavily weighted toward a small set of goods and services. Government, merely as consumer, exerts a powerful influence on the distribution of profits, wages, and wealth among industries. And as public expenditures increase relative to private consumption, government's distributional impact on the economy will increase as well.

In terms of federal purchases in 1970, $82.2 billion or 78 percent of a budgeted total of $105.6 billion was earmarked for the defense department. This 78 percent was heavily concentrated in a small number of industries, notably aerospace, electronics, ordinance, and transportation equipment. To a great extent these industries are part of the core economy precisely because of government intervention in the marketplace. The addition to an industry's total product demand, due to government purchases, often makes the difference between that industry rising into the core economy or being left behind in the periphery. None of the peripheral industries is noted for large defense contracts. Within the list of peripheral industries, only hospital services are significantly affected by government expenditures. Low wages in retail trade, personal services, and nondurable manufacturing, as well as in agriculture, are a function, in part, of government purchasing policy.

The application of federal corporate tax policy has also not been neutral. The corporation income tax has been constructed in such a way as to give maximum gain to the core economy. Liberalized depreciation and depletion allowances, investment credits, and other special tax write-offs favor the concentrated, capital-intensive, high profit industries of the core economy. The peripheral firms, when they realize a profit, are often taxed at higher rates than many industrial giants. Such a policy has had a significant and measurable effect on inter-industry wage differentials and wage increases over time.

In the past there has never been an explicit recognition of the public manipulation of wage differentials. The tripartite economy is *de facto* testimony, however, of the strategic role government plays in structuring individual industries and economic markets.[196]

The U.S. government also directly affects women's wages through the setting of "minimum wages." Two out of every three minimum-wage workers in America are women. Minimum wages are set by acts passed in the Senate and House of Representatives and must be signed by the president. Current and future minimum wages per hour are $2.65, 1978; $2.90, 1979; $3.10, 1980; and $3.35, 1981. Women or men who work over 40 hours a week are to be paid at 1½ times their regular pay. Waitresses, hotel employees, and other workers who rely on tips and earn $30 or more in tips per week must be paid 50 percent of the minimum wage with their tips serving in lieu of the remainder of their pay. In 1979, tips may be credited toward 45 percent of the minimum wage; in 1980, a 40 percent credit will be allowed. Employers who elect to use "tip credit" must have proof that they have informed their employees of their intention to do so.[197]

The Office of Management and Budget should publish yearly analyses of the impact of government spending on women's wages. It should examine the impact of government subsidies and tax credits on industries as well as minimum wage laws and federal employment programs.

An important related issue needing research is how blue-collar women are affected by credit rulings. Today credit is generally relied upon not only to increase the flexibility and usefulness of one's wages, but also to provide for basic necessities. The Equal Credit Opportunity Act, which was enacted by Congress in 1974, became effective in 1975, and was amended in 1976, has resulted in many women obtaining credit more easily. Especially important among the protections contained in the act is the regulation that a creditor cannot require a woman to reapply for a new account, change the terms of her account, or automatically close the account if she changes her name or marital status and has not relied solely on her spouse's income to receive credit. As the National Commission on the Observance of International Women's Year has pointed out, however, the Federal Reserve Board and other responsible agencies have yet to fully enforce the law, while many women have yet to learn of its provisions.[198] Researchers should explore whether blue-collar women have more difficulty than men or other women in obtaining loans. Those who study this credit issue should control for industry, income, race, and area of residence.

COMPANY, UNION, AND GOVERNMENT BENEFITS

Maternity Policies

October 31, 1978, President Carter signed Public Law 95-555 which stipulates that Title VII of the 1964 Civil Rights Act prohibits sex discrimination on the basis of pregnancy, childbirth or related medical complications.[199] The new law requires women affected by pregnancy, childbirth, or related medical conditions to be treated the *same* for all employment-related purposes, including receipt of benefits under fringe programs, as other persons not so affected but similar in their ability or inability to work.[200] According to an earlier Supreme Court ruling, Title VII of the Civil Rights Act does not permit the cancellation of accrued seniority of workers who return from childbirth leave.[201]

has continued to rise even though the number of children in the United States has declined substantially since 1970. Between March 1970 and March 1976, the number of children under age six whose mothers were in the labor force increased from 5.59 million to 6.4 million, while the total population of children under age six declined from 19.61 million to 17.64 million. The number of children aged six to seventeen with mothers in the labor force increased from 19.95 million to 21.72 million, while the total population aged six to seventeen declined from 46.15 million to 44.06 million. About 1.1 million of the preschoolers with working mothers were in female-headed families, 71 percent more than in 1970.[211]

Even though a woman works, she has not solved her childcare needs. A survey by the National Council of Jewish Women has found that thousands of American children are grossly neglected, living ten hours a day on their own, staying day after day at their mothers' places of work because no other arrangements can be made for them, or somehow surviving in childcare centers or family daycare homes of such poor quality that they may suffer lasting damage.[212] The childcare needs of workers vary by their familial, company, and union situations. In two cities, members of the Amalgamated Clothing Workers are offered outstanding childcare by their union, the only one with this service.[213] At the other extreme are thousands of postal, bank, maintenance, and factory workers who work at night and have neither childcare centers nor babysitters available to them. Because extensive research has already documented the severe childcare needs of these and other workers, more research is not required on the need itself. Rather, federally funded round-the-clock childcare should be established for the millions who need it, and research should be conducted to guide policymakers as to the types of childcare which should be established in various locales and for various workers.[214] The research should determine whether parents prefer child center care or stipends for home or family care; a center near their home or their workplace; or a community-, union-, or company-run center. What forms of childcare do workers of various ethnic backgrounds want? What forms of care do parents want for infants and children of various ages? Preschool, after-school, and vacation care as well as care of temporarily ill children should be considered. Evaluation research should accompany the early development of the childcare programs, and policymakers should consider various combinations of company- union- and government-sponsored care.[215]

Even parents who have solved their childcare problems are faced with the problem of caring for temporarily ill children. Some countries give parents extra sick leave to care for children.[216] Although many parents might welcome this policy, it could lead to increased employer discrimination against parents. Sweden has experimented with a system of "child visitors" who care for sick children in their own homes.[217] No conclusive research has been conducted on the effect upon children having child visitors rather than their own parents to care for them while they are ill. It would be important to know not only the answer to this question but also how many days should be allowed for child sick leave, and what policies parents and employers would prefer for the care of temporarily ill children.

Women who leave their jobs because their children are seriously but temporarily ill or lack a sitter during the night shift find that unemployment insurance (UI) offices treat their cases inconsistently. Unemployment insurance requires that workers who voluntarily leave their jobs must have "good cause" for doing so. Accoding to the UI service *Supplement on Women*, some states define a good cause to include personal circumstances, but twenty-eight states limit its meaning to job-related causes and exclude anyone who leaves work for personal reasons no matter how compelling. Moreover, as observed by Laura Perlman, many states disqualify workers (nearly always women) who voluntarily leave their jobs for family-related reasons from obtaining UI benefits for a period longer than the normal disqualification time for voluntary leaving; some disqualify until the women hold and lose another job. For voluntary leaving, the Department of Labor has recommended that UI programs pay the cost of all unemployment that is not the fault of the worker and that normal work availability requirements be adequate for deciding whether a person is unavailable for work.[218]

Retirement Needs

A decade or two after the children are raised, retirement presents itself. What economic and social problems will a woman face when she retires? Does she, like men, have an adjustment problem? How do her economic and social situations change as she ages? Researchers undertaking this study should control for whether the women are married, widowed, divorced, or never married as well as the number of years they worked prior to retirement and whether they belong to a union or company retirement group.[219] Even more important, the economic and pension situation of blue-collar single and married women should be studied. Because women live longer than men and inflation reduces the buying power of flat pensions, retired blue-collar women may experience greater economic hardships than blue-collar men.

Many small unionized as well as nonunionized plants have no pension plans at all. In 1971, only 36 percent of working women as compared with 52 percent of working men were covered by a union or company pension plan.[220] In addition, former Congresswoman Martha Griffiths has pointed out that even those women who are lucky enough to receive pensions receive considerably lower benefits than men. To illustrate, she writes:

> . . . in 1970 the median annual private pension for men was $2,080 and for women, $970. Low wages lead not only to low pensions but also to low social security payments. Women's median monthly Social Security payment in 1972 was $133, compared with $189 for men. Forty-two percent of the women received less than $120 per month, but only 19 percent of male beneficiaries received less than this amount.[221]

Many workers need to be told of the importance of pensions because it is more likely that they will be the first in their families to live beyond age sixty-five. More importantly, a national policy needs to be designed and instituted that provides all older persons with decent living conditions.

Social security, which covered more than twice as many persons as did employer-employee retirement plans in 1972, still discriminates against working women.[222] Unlike private pension plans, monthly social security payments are based on a woman's marital status and her previous earnings. Consequently, many women workers are shocked to learn upon retiring that because they are married and their income does not amount to more than half of their husband's, they are classified as dependents of their husbands. If married, the couple will receive a smaller income than if they were not married.[223] In other words, many wives will receive the same benefits whether they do or do not work. Numerous proposals have been made to correct this inequity; however, to date, no legislation has been passed. Although women are not excluded from social security coverage, they receive lower payments than men. As described earlier, social security benefits are based directly on covered earnings; however, women's earnings average only three-fifths of those received by men.

COMMUNITY SERVICES

Most community services—medical clinics, family services, and employment agencies—overlook women who are filling dual roles. These women, like working men, need weekend and weeknight services.[224] Many services have yet to be tailored to the lifestyles and desires of women and working-class people. Representatives of the ethnic and community group performing specific services should be hired as consultants to guide both the construction of community services and the professionals who work in them. The consultants should ensure that services meet the needs of the community and that people feel comfortable in using the services.[225] In addition, the working woman must act as an influence on these services. For example, would she be unable to influence her child's school or the neighborhood center if meetings were scheduled only during her working hours?

Researchers and community service professionals have yet to address the new phenomenon of high divorce rates among working-class women. Most local priests who serve as general helpers within blue-collar communities will not help women with divorce problems. Many women are also abandoned by their own families during this difficult time. Blue-collar women need friendship, help, and good counseling during and after divorce. Momma, a self-help organization having little financial support, helps women confront the combined problems of sex discrimination and single parenthood. The women and Momma need the support of all available community services and friends. Research should consider how counseling might best be geared to the needs and lifestyles of these and other blue-collar women and men who, for numerous economic and social reasons, differ from counselors' typical upper-middle-class clientele. A few studies similar to that by Lillian Rubin (see chapt. 2) have begun; however, many more are needed in order that counselors may learn to serve adequately persons of various ethnic, geographical, and economic groups.

Men and women also deserve adequate mental health services.[226] Today, most working-class men and women rely on over-the-counter drugs to treat nervous tension, depression, and neurotic symptoms until they become severely ill and require hospitalization. Throughout the nation, psychiatric and psychological services should be geared to meet the needs of working-class poor as well as upper-middle and upper-class persons. Research on mental health needs among various blue-collar ethnic and geographic groups could reveal how counselors, psychiatrists, and psychologists could better assist this clientele.

As with mental health care, general health care for working-class women and their families desperately needs revamping. Middle-class women, outraged by inadequate, chauvinistically delivered medical care, have been turning to self-help.[227] Working-class women too often have simply no health care. Research, perhaps conducted in conjunction with the CLUW or the National Congress of Neighborhood Women, could reveal alternative forms of health care that would be most appealing and of greatest use to working-class women.[228]

Efficient public transportation is another community service need of employed blue-collar women. Many women could earn more money waitressing or doing other jobs at night, but their realistic fears about the journey to and from work prevent them from taking the better paying night-shift work. Overall, black women have the most serious transportation difficulties. The Parnes national study of women aged thirty to forty-four found that blacks were more dependent upon public transportation for commuting to and from work (24 percent of black women as compared with 6 percent of white women) or driving with someone else (17 percent as compared with 7 percent). Most white women traveled to and from work in their own cars (65 percent as compared with 37 percent of black women). In addition, the Parnes study found that for every mode of travel, black women spent more time commuting than whites.[229]

ATTITUDES OF HUSBANDS

Many men in the Lordstown wildcat strike could hold out as long as they did because their wives were employed and they could stay home and care for the children. Such independence and a better standard of living are benefits that husbands receive because their wives work. On the other hand, some husbands of working women feel deprived of the special attention and extra care they would get if their wives were not working. Others feel their position threatened when their wives share in "bringing home the bacon." As Patricia and Brendon Sexton point out, most men have no choice; wives work so that the family may have an adequate standard of living.[230]

Little is known about the dynamics of blue-collar marriages in which wives and mothers work. Marriage counselors and others would be helped if an updated version of Mirra Komarovsky's *Blue-Collar Marriage* were published.[231] Blue-collar couples could be assisted by movies and television programs showing how other dual-career working-class couples cope. Their children could feel more normal if basic readers and children's books portrayed "mommies" as factory workers, grocery clerks, bus drivers, and hospital aides.

POLITICIZING THE ISSUES

The research and policy issues discussed in this paper were gathered primarily from organizationally active blue-collar employed women and their union and governmental representatives. Because of the unavailability of data on the majority of employed working-class women, their greatest needs, frustrations and hopes, as well as the extent of their support of women's issues in elections, are not known. This information should be gathered to demonstrate the needs of these women and to raise the awareness of politicians, union leaders, educators, and community service professionals.

CHAPTER 6. POLICIES AFFECTING
ATTITUDES OF BLUE-COLLAR EMPLOYED WOMEN

In the study described in chapter 2, Social Research, Inc., found that most working-class women supported the principles of equal pay for equal work and equal occupational opportunities for women and men. It is not known, however, how aware employed working-class women are of their legal employment rights or of information on affirmative action efforts of the CLUW, unions, and/or companies. Adequate information is not available on what work means to women of various occupational and ethnic groups. Indepth questionnaires, such as that used in Harold Sheppard and Neal Herrick's study on white male union workers, *Where Have All the Robots Gone?*, should be administered to women as well as men.[232]

Informally gathered information on the attitudes of many blue-collar employed women is presented through interviews of various women who expressed their concern. Ruth Weyland, associate general counsel of the International Union of Electrical, Radio and Machine Workers, wonders how women in her union can come to understand that income inequality between the sexes is unfair. She notes that the women are morally incensed about the lack of maternity benefits and maternity leave, but do not have the same feelings about income inequities.[233] West coast organizers for the United Electrical Workers express heartache when hearing about dozens of women electrical workers in their 20s confidently saying, "I won't be working long—only until we pay for the washer and dryer (the car, our vacation, etc.)—I don't need to worry about how this job's treating me." The organizers know that many women workers in their 40s and 50s held the same beliefs twenty years ago, and there is no reason to believe that these young women will not work most or all of the next thirty years. Other activists lament the plight of women who have families to support but have realistic fears of losing their jobs should they express their grievances.

Rose Beard, president of the UAW Women's Committee for regions I, IA, IB, and IE and an inspector in the sewing division of the Ford Motor Company's Ypsilanti plant, is concerned that many rank-and-file women are unwilling to work for forewomen as they do for foremen. She also pointed out that women must be taught not only to make grievances so that they can move up to better jobs, but not to work twice as hard in their new jobs as men. For example, she notes that women in her plant were always excluded from cleanup, an "easy" job for men. Now that women have obtained cleanup jobs, they are exhausted because they clean the plant as if it were their home.[234]

Numerous employers and union representatives asked, "How do you give women the confidence to break into a job traditionally held by men when they know about the job and their legal rights to it, and they believe they can do the job?" Several unionists asked, "How can we quickly wake women up to their own value so that they will have pride in being nurses aides; so that they will realize that electronics work is really not unskilled?" They observe that women must have this pride in order to fight for equitable pay.

To say that these attitudes simply reflect "the way these women are" would be "blaming the victim" and ignoring most social-psychological literature.[235] Personal attitudes are shaped by experiences, families, schooling, friends, occupational role models, and the opportunity structure of the job itself.[236] Based on the findings of an internal study by the International Union of Electrical Workers, which has organized many women's conferences and has in numerous ways worked diligently to raise women's awareness of their rights and to obtain these rights, their members report that "we now know our rights" and "men know we can do more than make sandwiches for the union."[237]

The establishment of various policies not only could assist women in developing job-specific attitudes and behaviors but also further their occupational advancement. Before discussing these policies and policy experiments, however, it must be noted that many women have already begun to change their outlook and behavior. Some have been proud of and happy with the changes; others have been confused by or displeased with what it has done to their marriages.[238] These findings suggest that the initiation of any demonstration research or social policies intended to change attitudes and behavior must be carried out carefully, by devoting attention to the project's impact on the women's sense of self, marital situation, and friendships, as well as on their work attitudes.

Women's support groups, in which thousands of middle-class women now participate, could be used in industrial plants of working-class communities and chapters of the CLUW or in organizing nonunionized women. The principle of support groups is simple: Out of the six to ten women in the group, one woman is responsible for convening the group and time is shared equally among all the group's members. Each woman begins by sharing some of the things she likes best about being a woman, some of her distressing experiences as a woman, and what she has done, is doing, and plans to do to alleviate the distressing aspects and increase the pleasant aspects of her life.[239] Given the information provided by this sharing, the group's convenor and other members may develop plans for the group to focus on more experience sharing of a general nature or on specific areas of concern in the future.

Numerous other activities might supplement women's support groups in an effort to encourage blue-collar women to realize their own value and to bid for better-paying jobs. The experience of women who enter traditionally male occupations should continue to be reported in union literature, women's magazines, local and high school newspapers, and television. Women will thereby be informed of changing occupational structure. Employers concerned with affirmative action should also be interviewed about new opportunities for women in their companies, and, in addition, circulate up-to-date literature on those opportunities. The story of today's working women should be developed and distributed to high school and working women so that they will become aware that they are likely to work most of their adult years and that it will be worth their while to seek equal pay and better jobs. The history of working women should also be developed and distributed so that women will understand their positions and take greater pride in their work.

Employers attempting to fulfill affirmative action goals might provide plant tours for women employees in low-paying jobs to show them better-paying positions within the plant. Short training programs could follow the tours to further demystify high-paying, traditionally male jobs and encourage women who might be interested in them. High school students could be given similar tours through several large plants in their community to learn that there are better- and poorer-paying jobs in every plant just as there are better- and poorer-paying industries. Insecurity arising from lack of experience, skills, or familiarity with the job market prevents some women from looking for jobs and others from looking further than the first job. Other women limit their job search to generally low-paid work mentioned by friends. In order to overcome these problems, the United States might experiment with policies similar to that of Sweden, where women who have spent several years at home raising their families have a right to government-subsidized training and a special training allowance to cover childcare and other expenses.[240]

Television should be used to inform women of better-paying job opportunities and help overcome insecurities that could prevent women from seeking jobs. Nancy Seifer recommends that:

- Television and radio programs affect the reality of working-class women's lives, and present characters who appeal to their aspirations and sense of dignity and with whom they can realistically and positively identify.
- Radio and television talk show discussions during both daytime and evening hours and articles in newspapers and magazines deal specifically with the changing roles of working-class women.
- Newspaper and magazine articles discuss legislative gains affecting all women, changes in the labor force, and new career opportunities for women without college educations.
- "How-to" features be developed by all the media on continuing education programs and job-training experiences, with concrete information on such programs' locations, eligibility requirements, costs, and benefits.
- Historical programs spotlight working-class women in leadership roles throughout the American experience, giving special attention to the struggles of immigrant and ethnic groups to affect societal and employment reforms.[241] In 1979, the National Commission on Working Women introduced Women at Work Broadcast Awards for the purpose of recognizing broadcasters performing in the public interest through exceptional reporting and programming on the concerns of working women, of promoting the development of programs and production ideas about working women; and of encouraging greater recognition of working women through an accurate portrayal of their lives.[242]

CHAPTER 7. UNIONS

THE POSITION OF WOMEN IN UNIONS

Eleven percent of all women in the labor force were union members in 1976.[243] Over three-quarters of these women were concentrated in twenty-one unions.[244] Although unionization appears to decidedly improve women's wages, women are affected by practices and policies that, in general, hinder unions and unionization as well as equal opportunity for both sexes.

Because the history of labor unions is not taught extensively in the public schools, women and men working in unorganized, nonunionized plants usually do not realize that benefits are missing. Readable elementary and high school texts are needed to explain the benefits of unionization to workers and to relate the history of labor's fight for social justice. The organizing of both women and men is hindered not only by the lack of public school education on labor, but also by the lack of laws similar to those enforced in Japan and Europe. These laws would limit the freedom of corporations to move without regard to the social impact that their move will have on the community. The lack of such laws also permits corporate employers to prevent unionization by threatening to move their plant when union organizing begins.[245]

The protection plan provided by the present National Labor Relations Act to employees attempting to unionize has weaknesses and severely affects women. In September 1977, numerous women's organizations testified before the House Subcommittee on Labor Management Relations in support of the passage of H.R. 8410, the Labor Law Reform Act of 1977, which is designed to give greater protection to employess attempting to unionize. Eleanor Smeal, president of NOW, pointed out, "The women of America probably have the most substantial stake in labor law reform. If we are ever to close the economic gap between men and women we must use the collective bargaining tool." She added, "The situation regarding the National Labor Relations Act is not unlike the situation regarding sex discrimination legislation: Although it has been on the books for over a decade, women have not been able to achieve equality in this nation due to the law's poor enforcement provisions and inadequate administration.[246] In addition, the delegates to the National Women's Conference held in November 1977 in Houston, Texas, passed the following resolution:

> The President should take into account in appointments to the National Labor Relations Board and in seeking amendments to the National Labor Relations Act of 1936 the obstacles confronting women who seek to organize in traditionally nonunionized employment sections.[247]

What positions are held by women within unions? In 1974, women comprised over 21 percent of the total union membership in the United States, and only 7 percent were union board members.[248] As of 1979, no women had ever served on the thirty-five-member executive council of the American Federation of Labor.[249]

All of the federation's thirteen departments, standing committees, trades departments and regional offices were headed by men in 1979.[250] Although 2.8 million women are AFL-CIO members, they are excluded from AFL-CIO vice-presidential positions because it is AFL-CIO policy to elect vice presidents from among heads of major international unions and no woman is in such a position.[251] Primarily as a consequence of Coalition of Labor Union Women activity, unions with large female memberships, such as the Communication Workers, the International Union of Electrical, Radio and Machine Workers, and the American Federation of State, County and Municipal Employees have increased their promotion of women staff members, have hired more women organizers and have supported more women's activities.[252] How might a larger proportion of women be brought into local, regional, and national positions of union leadership? First, more precise information is needed on women's participation in unions. Just as the Department of Labor develops a price index, Gloria Johnson suggest that it could develop an index of women's participation as elected and appointed officers for union use at the local, regional, and national levels.[253] The goal of unions should be to increase the percentage of women staff members and officers at all levels of the union hierarchy to compare favorably with the percentage of women at the local, regional, and national levels. Because information on the number of women in union locals by state is lacking, the Department of Labor should add a category on sex to its state breakdown of negotiated contracts.

Demonstration research projects and new policies accompanied by evaluation research should be initiated to promote women's full participation in union decisionmaking and election to higher-level local, regional, and national union offices. Many unions and various locals within the unions, like different professional associations and their constituent parts, bar women from full participation in varied ways. Therefore, studies similar to that by Wetheimer and Nelson in New York (see chapt. 2) should be conducted among various unions and ethnic groups of different regions in the nation. Following the studies, women's caucuses and the CLUW should monitor each union's progress in abolishing the barriers and fulfilling affirmative action goals.

Unions themselves could initiate change by increasing the percentage of women on their paid staffs. Unions could lead the way in job posting and other affirmative action steps suggested above for corporate employers. Unions might also sponsor courses on affirmative action for all leaders on local, regional, and national levels. The courses could include, for example, instructions on how to file a sex discrimination grievance against a company in behalf of a union member.

Unions could also help to change their members' attitudes concerning the role of women by greatly increasing the number of union newspaper and magazine articles devoted to women who are active in the union as well as explaining recent affirmative action laws. These articles could also focus on national and local activities of the CLUW, concerns of women's caucuses within unions, suggestions for how the union might better attain its affirmative action goals, up-to-date accounts of court cases affecting union women, and discussion conerning the position of union leaders to bargain for women's benefits, such as childcare, maternity leave, and various forms of job posting. The newspapers could also direct articles to union men on the importance of women's active participation in the union. Union leaders could ensure that a number of women address all union conventions.[254] An analysis of past union discussions and resolutions about women would reflect some of the basic attitudes, strengths, and problems in various unions' thinking concerning women—thinking which, while faulty, could be ahead of government legislation.

How can women be encouraged to play a more active, assertive role in their unions? Following the findings of the Wertheimer-Nelson study described above, both union and state college- or university-supported leadership training programs for women union members, including courses on public speaking, handling grievances, organizing, and collective bargaining, should be a high priority. Internship programs and other new forms of training should be established so that women may become expert at the more difficult skills of negotiating and handling grievances. The history of women's activities in union organizing and strikes should be emphasized to both men and women, thereby challenging the belief that women are harder to organize than men or contribute little to unions.

Although unions themselves practice sex discrimination, women union members are better off in terms of wages, benefits, and working conditions than most nonunionized women with similar jobs. Therefore, it is important to increase the percentage of women workers who are union members with union benefits.[255] Historically, unions have often attempted to organize plants having higher wages and fewer women, because the cost of organizing these plants will be rewarded with higher membership dues than can be obtained from lower-wage plants. Consequently, women have frequently been left unorganized or forced to organize themselves. The first step, of course, as pointed out by the CLUW statement of purpose, is for unions to devote an increased effort to organizing women. Research can aid these organizing efforts. A key question, "What are the best issues around which to organize unorganized women?," must be researched industry by industry and community by community.

UNIONS AND THE ENFORCEMENT OF
EQUAL OPPORTUNITY LAWS

To date, no study has been conducted on sexism in the labor negotiation process. The Bureau of Labor Statistics keeps on file all contracts of union agreements covering 1,000 or more workers. These are available to the public and should be scrutinized for sexually discriminatory matter. Researchers should investigate the degree to which the contracts were implemented in matters pertaining to affirmative action issues and examine the rulings made in sex arbitration cases. What are the bases for the rulings? Do the arbitration decisions take into account recent rulings by the EEOC? For all job areas, a demographic study using the bureau's statistical data should be conducted on the impact of women's wages and benefits. The study should control for the percentage of women union members, by occupation and geographical location.

In recent years, unions have found, usually much to their concern, that EEOC, the courts, employers, and other parties hold them responsible and financially liable for both inclusions and omissions in contract provisions negotiated by the unions as sole bargaining agents. Unions that have not represented fairly all members of their bargaining units in contract agreements are liable for the payment of legal fees and costs as well as back pay to the prevailing party.[256]

The discriminatory and unlawful work practice affecting the greatest number of workers concerns promotions, transfers, and layoffs that are determined by a worker's seniority within given units, where women and minorities are concentrated in the lowest paid of the units. Unions that did not initiate but allowed such practices to continue may be held financially liable for them. Hammerman and Rogoff of the EEOC report that while many internationals have adopted civil rights resolutions, few are programmatically specific, and fewer yet make headquarter commitments such as designation of a full-time staffperson. They recommend that all industrial unions include the following requirements in programs on equal employment opportunity:

- Adopt and publish a firm policy statement, by national convention, spelling out how the union intends to rid its industry of discrimination, and place full responsibility on the international for providing leadership, resources, and guidance in its implementation
- Establish machinery for gathering and evaulating information on employment practices in all companies and bargaining units on a continuing basis
- Require all locals, districts, and conference boards to negotiate contract provisions barring discrimination in employment and making EEO complaints grievable up through arbitration
- Require all locals to establish special committees to undertake immediate and continuous EEO review of collective bargaining agreements and employer work practices

- Assign to national full-time staff responsibility for fair practices activities
- Include a report of EEO progress and future plans on the agenda of every policymaking body and assembly, including international, district, and state conventions, international executive boards, joint boards, conference boards, and local unions
- Include instruction on Title VII and its implementation in all training programs, courses, seminars, and institutes for officers, members, and staff at all levels
- Ensure that all employee selection procedures (tests) conform to Title VII, including those unilaterally applied by employers as well as those within collective bargaining agreements and joint apprenticeship standards
- As an employer in its own right, apply the eight listed initatives to its own operations just as forcefully as it does in the industry with which it bargains[257]

TABLE 2

DISTRIBUTION OF FEMALES AND MALES IN VOCATIONAL EDUCATION
FOR EACH PROGRAM AREA, 1972

	Females			Males		
	Gainful, excluding home-making (%)	Including home-making (%)	N	Gainful (%)	(%)	Including home-making N
Agriculture	1	1	48,153	17	17	848,307
Distributive education	8	5	290,020	7	7	350,403
Health	8	4	285,071	1	1	51,581
Home economics, gainful	7	4	240,948	0.1	0.1	39,018
Office	51	28	1,796,387	11	11	555,491
Technical education	1	1	33,006	6	6	304,063
Trades/industry	8	4	279,680	43	43	2,118,288
Special program[*]	17	9	582,715	15	15	721,904
Total, gainful only	101		3,505,128	100—		4,931,284
Home economics, homemaking—	45		2,916,987	—0.5		248,745
Total gainful and homemaking	101		6,422,115	101		5,180,029

[*]Includes prevocational, pre-postsecondary, and remedial programs.

Source: Calculated from Bureau of Adult, Vocational and Technical Education, "Summary Data: Vocational Education, Fiscal Year 1972" (Washington, D.C.: U.S. Department of Health, Education, and Welfare, Office of Education, May 1973), p. 2.

SECTION III

CONCLUSION

WORKING CONDITIONS AND THE U.S. ECONOMY

Basic changes will be required in the economy before living conditions of blue-collar women are greatly improved. These changes involve vastly reducing the inequality in the distribution of our resources within our society and providing adequate employment for everyone.[258] During the process of working for these changes, many reforms should be made in policies affecting the living conditions of women in blue-collar jobs. This study has described many policy changes to be made and research projects to be conducted that relate to the conditions of these women and their families.

RESEARCH PRIORITIES

Foundations and government granting agencies are beginning to respond to the energy of the women's liberation movement as it relates to working-class issues by seeking and funding projects relevant to women employed in blue-collar jobs. All the research and policies recommended are needed. But because funding will be limited relative to the need, research priorities must be established. In the preceding chapters, possible negative consequences as well as benefits that could result from recommended policies and research were discussed. In addition to these considerations, the following criteria are recommended for determining research priorities:

- The number of women whose living conditions could be improved by the proposed research or policy change
- The degree of improvement of women's living conditions
- The relative need of the prospective population
- Implementation of the improvements in the most efficient and feasible manner

- The researcher's connections with relevant change agents
- The complexity of the proposed research
- The extent to which the research process could raise the consciousness of the target population in regard to their general economic and social needs
- The type of broad societal changes required to meet those needs

The dissemination of information about and the development and implementation of policies in line with our research findings are as important as our studies themselves. I encourage researchers who pursue policy-relevant studies to share their findings with the Coalition of Labor Union Women, the National Commission on Working Women, the National Congress of Neighborhood Women, and other advocates for blue-collar women, and with legislatures and relevant government, company, and union officials.

NOTES

1. The data for 1940 are for women 14 years and over; the data for 1979 are for women 16 years and over. Women's Bureau, U.S. Department of Labor, "1969 Handbook on Women Workers," Washington, D.C.: U.S. Government Printing Office, 1969, p. 92; Office of the Secretary, Women's Bureau, U.S. Department of Labor, "Women in the Labor Force: Annual Average 1979-1978," Washington, D.C.: stencil, February 1980, p. 2.

2. Women's Bureau, ibid., p. 2. Data include all races other than white; Spanish-speaking persons are included in the white population.

3. Ibid.; Robert Lindsey, "Women Entering Job Market at an 'Extraordinary' Pace," *New York Times*, September 12, 1976, p. 1; Bureau of Labor Statistics, U.S. Department of Labor, *Employment and Earnings* 27 (1): 171, January 1980.

4. U.S. Department of Labor, Office of the Secretary, Women's Bureau, "20 Facts on Women Workers," Washington, D.C.: U.S. Department of Labor, 1979, p. 1. In 1975, 1 million women received divorces. Only 14 percent of these women were awarded child support, fewer received alimony, and child support payments were generally less than half enough to support the children. National Commission on the Observance of International Women's Year, *"To Form a More Perfect Union": Justice for American Women*, Washington, D.C.: U.S. Government Printing Office, 1976, p. 57. In 1974, 4 million families with children were headed by females. Isabel Sawhill, "Discrimination and Poverty Among Women Who Head Families," *Signs* 1(3):203; cf. Heather Ross and Isabel Sawhill, *Time of Transition: The Growth of Families Headed by Women*, Washington, D.C.: The Urban Institute, 1975; Beverly Johnson McEaddy, "Women Who Head Families: A Socioeconomic Analysis," *Monthly Labor Review*, vol. 99, no. 6, June 1976.

5. U.S. Department of Labor, Women's Bureau, Ibid., p. 2; cf. Howard Hayge, "Families and the Rise of Working Wives," *Monthly Labor Review* 99(5):12-19, May 1976.

6. Bureau of the Census, U.S. Department of Commerce, "Money Income in 1977 of Families and Persons in the United States," *Current Population Reports*, ser. P-60, no. 118, March 1979, p. 236. Cf. Kathleen Shortridge, "Working Poor Women," *in* Jo Freeman (ed.), *Women: A Feminist Perspective*, Palo Alto, Calif.: Mayfield Publishing Company, 1975.

7. National Commission on Working Women. "Background Paper" and "Developing an Agenda for the First Year," Washington, D.C.: Center for Women and Work,

1977; National Commission on Working Women, *A Step Toward Equality: A Progress Report: September 1977-September 1978*, Washington, D.C.: U.S. Government Printing Office, 1979; National Commission on Working Women, *National Survey of Working Women: Perceptions, Problems and Prospects*, Washington, D.C.: Center for Women and Work, 1979. The National Commission on Working Women is headquartered at 1211 Connecticut Avenue, N.W./Suite 310, Washington, D.C. 20036; telephone 202-466-6770.

8. Cf. International Labour Office, *Women Workers: International Perspectives*, Geneva: International Labour Office, 1976. Alice Cook has also done considerable research of a cross-national nature, which is reviewed below. In 1976, the German Marshall Fund solicited proposals for comparative research on women and work. For research related to rural women workers, see Colette H. Moser and Deborah Johnson, *rural Women Workers in the 20th Century: An Annotated Bibliography*, National Technical Information Service Report NTIS PB 226487/AS, 1973; and Kathryn F. Clarenback, "Educational Needs of Rural Women and Girls," Washington, D.C.: National Advisory Council on Women's Educational Programs, 1977.

9. Rosabeth Kantor, *Work and Family in the United States: A Critical Review and Agenda for Research and Policy*, New York: Russell Sage Foundation, 1976; a White House conference on families is to be held in 1979.

10. C. Wright Mills, *White Collar*, New York: Oxford University Press, 1956, pp. 208-209.

11. Cf. Jean Tepperman, *Not Servants, Not Machines: Officeworkers Speak Out*, Boston: Beacon Press, 1976; Mary Kathleen Benet, *The Secretarial Ghetto*, New York: McGraw-Hill, 1972; Margery Davies, "Woman's Place Is at the Typewriter: The Feminization of the Clerical Labor Force," *Radical America* 8:1-28, July/August 1974; Evelyn Nakano Glenn and Roslyn L. Feldberg, "Degraded and Deskilled: The Proletarinization of Clerical Work," *Social Problems*, vol. 25, no. 1, October 1977; Roslyn L. Feldberg and Evelyn Nakano Glenn, "Category or Collectivity? The Consciousness of Clerical Workers," a paper presented at the Society for the Study of Social Problems, Chicago, 1977; Phyllis Marynick Palmer and Sharon Lee Grant, *The Status of Clerical Workers: A Summary Analysis of Research Findings and Trends*, Washington, D.C.: Women's Studies Program, George Washington University, 1979; Women Employed Institute, *The Women in the Office: The Economic Status of Clerical Workers*, Chicago: Women Employed Institute, 1979.

12. The seventies have produced several landmark volumes concerning work and the conditions and consciousness of the working class as a whole. Cf. Harry Braverman, *Labor and Monopoly Capital: The Degradation of Work in the Twentieth Century*, New York: Monthly Review Press, 1974; Stanley Aronowitz, *False Promises: The Shaping of American Working Class Consciousness*, New York: McGraw-Hill, 1973; Andrew Levison, *The Working Class Majority*, New York: Penguin Books, 1974; Staughton and Alice Lynd, *Rank and File: Personal Histories by Working Class Organizers*, Boston: Beacon Press, 1973; Patricia Cayo Sexton and Brendon Sexton, *Blue Collars and Hard Hats: The Working Class and the Future of American Politics*, New York: Random House, 1971; Richard Sennett and Jonathan Cobb, *The Hidden Injuries of Class*, New York: Alfred A. Knopf, Inc., 1972.

13. The National Commission for the Observance of International Women's Year has made a similar recommendation, op. cit., pp. 103-104.

14. Among the many books which were published on women in working-class jobs during these early years are: Mable Hurd Willett, *The Employment of Women in the Clothing Trade*, New York: Columbia University Press, 1902; Edith Abbott, *Women in Industry: A Study in American Economic History, New York: D. Appleton and Company, 1910; Olive Schreiner, Women and Labor*, New York: Stokes, 1911; Alice Henry, *Women and the Labor Movement*, New York: George H. Doran, 1923; Alice Henry, *The Trade Union Women*, New York: Appleton, 1915; Frances Donovan, *The Woman Who Waits* (about waitressing), Boston: R.G. Badger, 1920; Mary Van Kleeck, *A Seasonal Industry: A Study of the Millinery Trade*, New York: Russell Sage Foundation, 1917; Louise C. Odencrantz, *Italian Women in Industry*, New York: Russell Sage Foundation, 1919; Elizabeth Beardsley Butler, *Saleswomen in Mercantile Stores*, New York: Russell Sage Foundation/Survey Association, Inc., 1913; Amy Hewes, *Women as Munition Makers: A Study of Conditions in Bridgeport, Conn.*, New York: Russell Sage Foundation, 1917: U.S. Congress, *Report on Condition of Woman and Child Wage-Earners in the United States*, Senate, 61st Congress, 2d sess., doc. no. 645, 1910; National Federation of Settlements, *Young Working Girls*, New York: Houghton and Mifflin Co., 1913; Annie Marion MacLean, *Women Workers and Society*, Chicago: A.C. McClung and Co., 1916; Gwendolyn Salisbury Hughes, *Mothers in Industry: Wage Earning Women in Philadelphia*, New York: New Republic, Inc., 1925; Annie Marion MacLean, *Wage Earning Women*, New York: The Macmillan Co., 1910; Sue Ainslie Clark and Edith Wyatt, *Making Both Ends Meet: The Income and Outlay of New York Working Girls*, New York: The Macmillan Co., 1911; Helen Campbell, *Prisoners of Poverty: Women Wage-Workers, Their Trades and Their Lives*, Boston: Little, Brown and Company, 1900; Women's Educational and Industrial Union of Boston, *Studies in Economic Relations of Women: The Food of Working Women in Boston*, Boston: Wright and Potter, 1917; Mrs. John Van Vorst, *The Woman Who Toils; Being the Experiences of Two Gentlewomen as Factory Girls*, New York: Doubleday, Page and Co. 1903; Charles E. Persons, Mabel Parton, and Mabelle Moses, *Labor Laws and Their Enforcement*, New York: Longmans, Green and Co., 1911; Lorinda Perry, *The Millinery Trade in Boston and Philadelphia*, New York: The Vail-Ballou Co., 1916; Annette Man, *Women Workers in Factories*, Cincinnati: The Consumer's League of Cincinnati, 1918; Eleanor L. Lattimore and Ray S. Trent, *Legal Recognition of Industrial Women*, New York: Y.W.C.A. Industrial Commission, 1919; Meta Stern Lilenthal, *From Fireside to Factory*, New York: Rand School of Social Science, 1916; Katharine Anthony, *Mothers Who Must Earn: West Side Studies*, New York: Survey Associates, Inc., 1914; Mary Van Kleeck, *Artificial Flower Makers*, New York: Russell Sage Foundation/Survey Associates, Inc., 1923; Mary Van Kleeck, *Women in the Bookbinding Trade*, New York: Russell Sage Foundation/Survey Associates, Inc., 1913; Josephine Goldmark, *Fatigue and Efficiency: A Study of Industry*, New York: Russell Sage Foundation/Survey Associates, Inc., 1914; Edna Bryner, *Dressmaking and Millinery*, Cleveland: Cleveland Education Survey/The Survey Committee of the Cleveland Foundation, 1916; Iris Prout O'Leary, *Department Store Occupations*, Cleveland: The Survey Committee of the Cleveland Foundation, 1916; Lucile Eaves, *The Food of Working Women in Boston*, Boston: State Department of Health, Commonwealth of Massachusetts, 1917.

The U.S. Women's Bureau published the following studies on women in blue-collar and industrial jobs prior to 1925: "Wages of Candy Makers in Philadelphia in

1919," bull. 4, June 1919, 46 pp.; "Home Work in Bridgeport, Connecticut," bull. 9, December 1919, 38 pp.; "Hours and Conditions of Work for Women in Industry in Virginia," bull. 10, March 1910, 31 pp.; "Women Street Car Conductors and Ticket Agents," bull. 11, 1921, 89 pp.; "Health Problems of Women in Industry," bull. 18, May 1921, 11 pp.; "Negro Women in Industry," bull. 20, 1922, 65 pp.; "What Industry Means to Women Workers," bull. 31, 1923, 10 pp.; "Radio Talks on Women in Industry," bull. 36, 1924, 21 pp.

15. Cf. Leon Stein, *The Triangle Fire*, New York: J.B. Lippincott Co., 1962; Joyce Maupin, *Working Women and Their Organizations: 150 Years of Struggle*, Berkeley, Calif.: Union WAGE, 1974; Rosalyn Baxandall, Linda Jordon, and Susan Reverby (eds.), *America's Working Women: A Documentary History - 1600 to the Present*, New York: Vintage Books, 1976; Barbara Wertheimer, *We Were There: The Story of Working Women in America*, New York: Random House, in press; Alice Henry, *The Trade Union Woman*, op. cit.

16. For more general analyses of the influence of elite social reformers on government social programs for the poor, see Gabriel Kolko, *The Triumph of Conservatism*, Chicago: Quadrangle Books, 1963; James Weinstein, *The Corporate Ideal in the Liberal State 1900-1918*, Boston: Beacon Press, 1968; Martin J. Sklar, "Woodrow Wilson and the Political Economy of Modern United States Liberalism," *in* James Weinstein and David W. Eakins (eds.), *For a New America: Essays in History and Politics*, New York: Random House, 1970; Anthony M. Platt, *The Child Savers, The Invention of Delinquency*, Chicago: University of Chicago Press, 1969.

17. Cf. quotations in Pamela Roby (ed.), *The Poverty Establishment*, Englewood Cliffs, N.J.: Prentice-Hall, 1974: Charles Burroughs, 1835, p. 6; Josephine Shaw Lowell, 1884, p. 115; Charity Organization of New York, p. 115; S. Humphreys Gurteen, 1879, p. 169; New York Association for Improving the Condition of the Poor, 1856, p. 169.

18. Cf. C. Wright Mills, "The Professional Ideology of Social Pathologists," *American Journal of Sociology*, vol. 49, 1943; for a broader analysis of the conditions of more well-to-do women, see Pamela Roby, "Women and American Higher Education," *The Annals of the American Academy of Political and Social Science* 404:118-139, November 1972.

19. James Weinstein, *The Corporate Ideal in the Liberal State 1900-1918*, op. cit., p.x.

20. Among the many general texts which focus exclusively or nearly exclusively on men and overlook women's occupational concerns are the following 50 volumes: Henry Borow, *Man in a World at Work*, Boston: Houghton Mifflin, 1964; Sigmund Nosow and William H. Form, *Man, Work and Society: A Reader in the Sociology of Occupations*, New York: Basic Books, 1962; Everett C. Hughes, *Men and Their Work*, Glencoe: The Free Press, 1958; Nels Anderson, *Dimensions of Work: The Sociology of a Work Culture*, New York: David McKay Co., Inc., 1964; Peter L. Berger, *The Human Shape of Work: Studies in the Sociology of Occupations*, New York: Macmillan, 1964; Theodore Caplow, *The Sociology of Work*, New York: McGraw-Hill, 1954; Delbert C. Miller and William H. Form, *Industrial Sociology: The Sociology of Work Organizations*, New York: Harper and Row, 1964; Seymour Wolfbein, *Work in American Society*, Glenview, Illinois: Scott, Foresman and Co., 1971; Stanley Parker, *The Future of Work and Leisure*, New York: Praeger, 1971; Erwin O. Smigel (ed.), *Work and Leisure*, New York: College and University Press,

1963; Lee Taylor, *Occupational Sociology*, New York: Oxford University Press, 1968; Fred Best, *The Future of Work*, Englewood Cliffs, N.J.: Prentice-Hall, 1973; Clifton D. Bryant, *Social Dimensions of Work*, Englewood Cliffs, N.J.: Prentice-Hall, 1972; Carl B. Kaufman, *The Individual and His Work in Organized Society*, New York: Doubleday, 1969; Alan Kraus (ed.), *The Nature of Work*, New York: Wiley, 1972; Joseph H. Oldham, *Work in Modern Society*, New York: John Knox, 1961; Yves Sem, *Work, Society and Culture*, New York: Fordham, 1971; Walter L. Slocum, *Occupational Careers: Sociological Perspectives*, Chicago: Aldine, 1966; S.R. Parker et al., *The Sociology of Industry*, New York: Praeger, 1967; E.V. Schneider, *Industrial Sociology*, New York: McGraw-Hill, 1969; Wilbert E. Moore, *Industrial Relations and the Social Order*, New York: Macmillan, 1946; Robert Dubin, *The World of Work*, New York: Prentice-Hall, 1958; Edward Gross, *Work and Society*, New York: Crowell, 1958; Arthur B. Shostak and William Gomberg (eds.), *Blue Collar World*, Englewood Cliffs, N.J.: Prentice-Hall, 1964; Patricia Cayo Sexton and Brendon Sexton, *Blue Collars and Hard Hats*, New York: Random House, 1971; Georges Freedman, *The Anatomy of Work: Labor, Leisure and the Implications of Automation*, New York: Free Press, 1961; Daniel Bell, *Work and Its Discontents*, Boston: Beacon Press, 1954; William A. Faunce, *Readings in Industrial Sociology*, New York: Appleton, 1967; William A. Faunce, *Problems of an Industrial Society*, New York: McGraw-Hill, 1968; W.F. Whyte (ed.), *Industry and Society*, New York: McGraw-Hill, 1946; Reinhard Bendix, *Work and Authority in Industry*, New York: Wiley, 1956; Arthur Kornhauser, Robert Dubin, and Arthur Ross (eds.), *Industrial Conflict*, New York: McGraw-Hill, 1954; Tom Burns (ed.), *Industrial Man*, Baltimore: Penguin, 1969; Bernard M. Bass and Gerald V. Barrett, *Man, Work and Organizations: An Introduction to Industrial and Organizational Psychology*, Boston: Allyn and Bacon, Inc., 1972; Leonard R. Sayles, *Behavior of Industrial Work Groups*, New York: Wiley, 1958; Lloyd H. Lofquist and Rene V. Davies, *Adjustment to Work: A Psychological View of Man's Problems in a Work-Oriented Society*, New York: Appleton, 1969; A. Korman, *Industrial and Organizational Psychology*, Englewood Cliffs, N.J.: Prentice-Hall, 1971; A. Fraser Isbester, *Industry and Labor Relations*, Boston: Heath, 1967; Gerald G. Somers (ed.), *Essays in Industrial Relations Theory*, Ames: Iowa State University Press, 1969; Conrad Arensberg et al. (eds.), *Research in Industrial Human Relations*, New York: Harper, 1957; Burleigh B. Gardner, *Human Relations in Industry*, Chicago: Irwin, 1945; Sar A. Levitan (ed.), *Blue Collar Workers*, New York: McGraw-Hill, 1971; Eli Ginzberg and H. Berman, *The American Worker in the Twentieth Century*, New York: Free Press, 1963; Gary Becker, *Human Capital*, New York: National Bureau of Economic Research, 1964; William Bowen, *The Economics of Labor Force Participation*, Princeton: Princeton University Press, 1969; Belton M. Fleisher, *Labor Economics: Theory and Evidence*, Englewood Cliffs, N.J.: Prentice-Hall, 1970; Lloyd G. Reynolds, *The Structure of Labor Markets*, New York: Harper and Row, 1951; Herbert S. Parnes, *Research on Labor Mobility*, New York: Social Science Research Council, 1954; Robert Aaron Gordon (ed.), *Toward a Manpower Policy*, New York: John Wiley and Sons, 1967; Lester C. Thurow, *Investment in Human Capital*, Los Angeles: Wadsworth, 1970.

21. Cf. F. J. Roethlisberger and W.J. Dickson, *Management and the Workers*, Cambridge, Mass.: Harvard University Press, 1939; W.F. Whyte, *Human Relations in the Restaurant Industry*, New York: McGraw-Hill, 1948: Henry A. Landsberger,

Hawthorne Revisited, New York: New York State School of Industrial and Labor Relations, 1948; Alex Carey, "The Hawthorne Studies: A Radical Criticism," *American Sociological Review*, vol. 32, no. 3, June 1967.

22. Cf. Charlotte Wolf, "Sex Roles as Portrayed in Marriage and Family Textbooks: Contributions to the Status Quo," mimeographed, Colorado Women's College, 1971; Carol Ehrlich, "The Male Sociologist's Burden: The Place of Women in Marriage and Family Texts," *The Journal of Marriage and the Family*, vol. 33, no. 3.

23. Mirra Komarovsky, *Blue-Collar Marriage*, New York: Random House, 1962, ch. 3: "The Homemaker and the Working Wife." No reference is made to the employed wife in Lee Rainwater, Richard P. Coleman, and Gerald Handel, *Workingman's Wife: Her Personality, World and Life Style*, New York: Macfadden Books, 1959.

24. The seven *American Journal of Sociology* articles were: Edith Abbott, "Women in Industry: The Manufacture of Boots and Shoes," *15*:335-360; Josephine C. Goldmark, "The Necessary Sequel of Child Labor Laws," *11*:312; Annie M. MacLean, "Factory Legislation for Women in the U.S.," *3*:721-741; Annie M. MacLean, "The Sweatshop in Summer," *9*:289-309; U.G. Weatherly, "How Does the Access of Women to Industrial Occupations React upon the Family?," *14*:740-765; Jane Addams, "Trade Unions and Public Duty," *4*:448-462.

25. J.R. Leevy, "The Modern Industrial Working Women," *American Sociological Review*, 8:720-722; Pamela Roby, "Sociology and Women in Working Class Jobs," *Sociological Inquiry*, vol. 45, no. 2-3, summer 1975.

26. *Prodeedings of the Twenty-Fifth Annual Winter Meeting and Index of IRRA Publications 1966-1973*, Madison, Wis.: Industrial Relations Research Association, 1973, pp. 468-487.

27. The following similarly ignored women wokers: Gerald G. Somers (ed.), *The Next Twenty-Five Years of Industrial Relations*, Madison, Wis.: Industrial Relations Research Association, 1973; Neil H. Chamberlain, Frank C. Pierson, and Theresa Wolfson, *A Decade of Industrial Relations Research, 1946-1956*, New York: Harper, 1958.

28. Union WAGE has grown considerably since its founding and through its bimonthly newspaper, *Union WAGE*, has influence far beyond its seven West Coast chapters.

29. Cf. "Women Unionists Discuss Activism, 600 Meet Here to Demand Leadership Roles," *New York Times*, January 20, 1974, p. 52; Gretchen Donart, "No More Ladies' Auxiliary," *The Democratic Left*, vol. 2, no. 1, January 1974; Beth Alexander, "Working Women Are on the Move," *World Magazine*, March 9, 1974, p. 2.

30. *National Congress of Neighborhood Women*, issue no. 1, June 1974, and issue no. 2, August 1974.

31. Cf. Patricia Cayo Sexton, "Workers (Female) Arise! On Founding the Coalition of Labor Union Women," *Dissent 21* (3):380-395, summer 1974; Eileen Shanahan, "3,000 Delegates at Chicago Meeting Organize a National Coalition of Labor Union Women," *The New York Times*, March 25, 1974, p. 27; Connie Kopelov, *Trade Union Women and Women's Rights*, Cambridge, Mass.: M.A. thesis, Goddard College, August 9, 1974, ch. 4, "New York Trade Union Women's Conference," and ch. 5, "Coalition of Labor Union Women;" Annemarie Troger, "Coalition of Labor Union Women: Strategic Hope, Tactical Despair," *Radical America 9* (6):111-114, November 1975; Ann Withorn, "The Death of CLUW," *Radical America 10* (2):47-51, March 1976; "Ms. Blue-Collar," *Time*, May 6, 1974, p. 80; "Women Push for Union Power," *Business Week*, March 30, 1974, p. 102; "Women Rig CLUW

Conference," *Workers Vanguard*, March 15, 1974, p. 12; "Working Women Demand 'Equal Pay for Equal Work.'" *United Labor Action 4* (3):1, March 18, 1974; Alan Merridew, "Union Women Organizing Coalition," *Chicago Tribune*, March 24, 1974, p. 33; Anne Lipow et al., "A Giant Step Forward," Joyce Maupin, "Rank and File Victory," and Kay Eisenhower, "Open Membership," *Union WAGE*, no. 23, May-June 1974, pp. 4-5; Elizabeth McRide, "Labor's 'Special Problem,'" and Heather Booth, "Liberation and Social Change," *The Democratic Left 2* (4):3-5, April 1974.

32. Cf. Rex Hardesty, "Farah: The Union Struggle of the 70's," *The American Federationist*, June 1973; Gerri Pressnall, "Viva La Huelga," *Battle Acts 3* (1):24-25; Barbara Teel, "Chicano Workers Seek Union at Farah Slacks," *Workers World*, October 6, 1972, p. 2; "Boycott Farah! Strike 18 Months Old," *Union WAGE*, no. 2, November 1973, p. 1; "Women Electronics Workers Strike for Living Wages in Concord," *San Francisco Bay Guardian*, May 11-24, 1974, p. 2; "Electronic Shock Waves," *San Francisco Bay Guardian*, June 22, 1974, p. 2.

33. The conference is also briefly summarized in *Women in Blue-Collar Jobs: A Ford Foundation Report*, New York: The Ford Foundation, 1976. The conference's major policy recommendation was the establishment of a National Task Force and Office on Wage-Earning Women to conduct hearings on specific subjects of concern to women in the work force (for example, the dilemma of seniority rights versus affirmative action during recession layoffs); hold regional conferences for the growing numbers of those engaged in research on wage-earning women; bring researchers and blue-collar and service industry women together for dialogues on what reasearch is most needed; encourage more minority women in the academic world to move into research in this area; develop a program of fellowships for minority women as one mode of encouragement; and inform the U.S. Congress, state and local policymakers, employers, and unions of recent findings concerning the conditions and needs of wage-earning women. The National Commission on Working Women and the National Center for Women and Work grew directly out of these recommendations. Susan Berresford of the Ford Foundation greatly assisted both efforts.

34. For a report on research on women and all areas of work conducted by the Office of Research and Development of the Employment and Training Administration of the U.S. Department of Labor, see Patricia Cayo Sexton, *Women and Work*, R&D Monograph no. 46, U.S. Department of Labor, Washington, D.C.: U.S. Government Printing Office, 1977.

35. Sally Hillsman Baker, *Entry into the Labor Market: The Preparation and Job Placement of Negro and White Vocational High School Graduates*, unpublished Ph.D. dissertation, Columbia University, 1970.

36. Sally Hillsman Baker and Bernard Levenson, "Job Opportunities of Black and White Working-Class Women," *Social Problems 22* (4):519-520, April 1975.

37. Ibid., p. 522.

38. Sally Hillsman Baker and Bernard Levenson, "Earnings Prospects of Black and White Working-Class Women," a paper presented at the Annual Meeting of the American Sociological Association, San Francisco, California, August 1975.

39. Phyllis A. Wallace, *Pathways to Work: Unemployment among Black Teenage Females*, Lexington, Mass.: Lexington Books, 1974.

40. Manpower Administration, U.S. Department of Labor, *Women in Apprenticeship— Why Not?*, Manpower Research Monograph no. 33, Washington D.C.: U.S.

Government Printing Office, 1974. Interview with Norma Briggs, January 3, 1974.

41. San Francisco Advocates for Women, Dorothy Hernandez, Director, 564 Market Street, San Francisco, California.

42. Better Jobs for Women, Sandy Carruthers, Director, 1543 Tremont Place, Denver, Colorado 80202 (303/244-4189). Interview with Pamela Williams, May 14, 1974.

43. Mary Lindenstein Walshok, "Nontraditional Blue-Collar Work Among Urban Women," a paper presented at the Annual Meeting of the American Sociological Association, San Francisco, California, August 1975; Walshok, "Women and Work: Expanding Employment Opportunity for Women in an Urban Society," a proposal submitted for National Institute of Mental Health, grant no. IRol Mh2768-01, 1974.

44. Women in professional and managerial positions expressed a greater willingness to work: 74 percent of white women and 76 percent of black women in professional or managerial occupations said that they would continue to do so in the absence of financial need. Herbert S. Parnes, John R. Shea, Ruth S. Spitz, and Frederick A. Zeller, *Dual Careers: A Longitudinal Study of Labor Market Experience of Women*, vol. 7, Washington, D.C.: U.S. Government Printing Office, 1970, p. 174 (Parnes Study, prepared for Manpower Administration, U.S. Department of Labor).

45. "Good wages" was the reply given by 32 percent of the white and 49 percent of the black blue-collar workers and 22 percent of the white and 38 percent of the black nondomestic service workers. Panes et al., op. cit., p. 180.

46. Parnes et al., op. cit., p. 185.

47. Nondomestic service workers cited coworkers (9 percent) and hours (7 percent) next. Parnes et al., op. cit., p. 192.

48. Manpower Administration, U.S. Department of Labor, *Job Satisfaction: Is This a Trend?*, Manpower Research Monograph no. 30, Washington, D.C.: U.S. Government Printing Office, 1974, p. 10; Frederick Herzberg, Bernard Mausner, Richard Peterson, and Dora Carpwell, *Job Attitudes: Review of Research and Opinion*, Pittsburgh: Psychological Services of Pittsburgh, 1957.

49. Manpower Administration, U.S. Department of Labor, *Job Satisfaction*, op cit., p. 18.

50. Laura Lein, Center for Research on Women, Wellesley College, Wellesley, Mass. 02181. Interview, May 12, 1974.

51. Laura Lein, Maureen Durham, Michael Pratt, Michael Schudson, Ronald Thomas, and Heather Weiss, *Work and Family Life*, final report, National Institute of Education Project No. 3-3094, Cambridge, Mass.: Center for the Study of Public Policy, 1974, p. 160.

52. Ibid., pp. 162-163.

53. Ibid., p. 163.

54. Ibid., p. 165. Laura Lein, conversation, July 26, 1975.

55. Lillian Rubin, Professor, The Wright Institute, Berkeley, California, interview, May 15, 1974. Cf. Lillian Rubin, *Worlds of Pain: Life in the Working Class Family*, New York: Basic Books, 1976.

56. Lillian Rubin, Professor, The Wright Institute, at the First National Working Conference on Research on Women in Blue-Collar Jobs, New York: The Ford Foundation, December 5, 1974, typed transcript, pp. 148-149.

57. Mary Lou Finley, "The Class Consciousness and Sex Class Consciousness of Women Factory Workers: Research in Progress," a paper prepared for the First National

Working Conference on Research on Women in Blue-Collar Jobs, New York: The Ford Foundation, December 5-6, 1974, p. 4.

58. Myra Marx Ferree, research summary submitted to the First National Working Conference on Research on Women in Blue-Collar Jobs, New York: The Ford Foundation, December 5-6, 1974; Ferree, "Jobs for Women: Alienation or Liberation?" and "The Women's Movement in the Working-Social Class," chapters of a Ph.D. dissertation, Department of Psychology and Social Relations, supported in part by a grant from the Peter B. Livingston Research Fund, Harvard University.

59. Louise Lamphere, Center for Policy Research, New York City, letter, July 31, 1976.

60. Helena Z. Lopata, letter to Pamela Roby, February 13, 1978.

61. *Working-Class Women in a Changing World*, prepared for McFadden-Bartell Corp. (study 287107), Chicago: Social Research Inc., 1973, pp. 5, 9, 12.

62. Nancy Seifer, *Absent from the Majority: Working-Class Women in America*, New York: National Project on Ethnic America of the American Jewish Committee, 1973, 85 pp.

63. Nancy Seifer, *Nobody Speaks for Me!: Self-Portraits of American Working Class Women*, New York: Simon and Schuster, 1976.

64. Rachelle Barcus Warren, "The Work Role and Problem Coping: Sex Differentials in the Use of Helping Systems in Urban Communities," a paper presented at the Annual Meeting of the American Sociological Association, San Francisco, California, August 1975.

65. Alice H. Cook, *The Working Mother: A Survey of Problems and Programs in Nine Countries*, Ithaca: New York State School of Industrial and Labor Relations, Cornell University, 1975, pp. 30, 37; cf. Cook, "Working Women: European Experience and American Need," Joint Economic Committee of the United States, *American Women Workers in a Full Employment Economy*, September 15, 1977, 95th Congress, 1st sess.

66. Louise K. Howe, *Pink-Collar Worker*, New York: Putnam, 1976.

67. Press release, *University of Michigan News*, October 22, 1975. Also see the autobiographical accounts of women organizers Stella Nowicki and Sylvia Woods in Alice and Staughton Lynd (eds.), *Rank and File: Personal Histories by Working-Class Organizers*, Boston: Beacon Press, 1973. The film "Union Maids," based on the Lynds' book, is available from New Day films, P.O. Box 315, Franklin Lakes, New Jersey 07417 (201/891-8240).

68. Barbara Wertheimer and Anne H. Nelson, "The Changing Role of America's Working Women," stencil, p. 6; Wertheimer and Nelson, *Trade Union Women: A Study of Their Participation in New York City Locals*, New York: Praeger, 1975. For a summary of union self-studies about participation by their female members, see Barbara M. Wetheimer, "Search for a Partnership Role: Women in Labor Unions Today," in Jane Roberts Chapman (ed.), *Economic Independence for Women*, Beverly Hills, Calif.: Sage Publications, 1976. Barbara Wertheimer is Director and Anne Nelson is Associate Director of Trade Union Women's Studies, New York State School of Labor and Industrial Relations, Cornell University, 7 East 43d Street, New York, New York 10017; for statistics on women union members and women union leaders, see Lucretia Dewey, "Women in Labor Unions," *Monthly Labor Review*, vol. 94, February 1971; Edna E. Raphael, "Working Women and Their Membership in Labor Unions," *Monthly Labor Review*, vol. 97, no. 5, May 1974; Virginia A.

Berquist, "Women's Participation in Labor Organizations," *Monthly Labor Review*, vol. 97, no. 10, October 1974. Also see Gail Falk, "Sex Discrimination in the Trade Unions: Legal Resources for Change," *in* Jo Freeman (ed.), op. cit., pp. 254-276; and Alice Cook, "Women and Amercian Trade Unions," *Annals of the American Academy of Political and Social Science*, vol. 375, January 1968.

69. Interview, May 14, 1975. See Jeanne M. Stellman, *Women's Work, Women's Health: Myth and Realities*, New York: Pantheon Books, 1977; and Jeanne M. Stellman and Susan M. Daum, *Work Is Dangerous to Your Health: A Handbook of Health Hazards in the Workplace and What You Can Do About Them*, New York: Pantheon, 1973. Cf. Paul Brodeau, *Expendable Americans*, New York: Viking Press, 1973; Nicholas A. Ashford, "Worker Health and Safety: An Area of Conflicts," *Monthly Labor Review*, vol. 98, no. 9, September 1975; Rachel Scott, *Muscle and Blood*, New York: E.P. Dutton and Co., Inc., 1974; Franklin Wallick, *The American Worker: An Endangered Species*, New York: Ballantine Books, 1972; Andrea Hricko with Melanie Brunt, *Working for Your Life: A Woman's Guide to Job Health Hazards*, Berkeley, Calif.: Labor Occupational Health Program, 2521 Channing Way, 1976 ($8.00); Bruce L. Margolis and William H. Kroes, "Work and the Health of Man," James S. House, "The Effects of Occupational Stress on Physical Health," and Stanislav V. Kasl, "Work and Mental Health," *in* James O'Toole (ed.), *Work and the Quality of Life: Resource Papers for Work in America*, Cambridge, Mass.: The MIT Press, 1974; Special Task Force to the U.S. Secretary of Health, Education, and Welfare, *Work in America*, Cambridge, Mass.: The MIT Press, no date, ch. 3: "Work and Health."

70. Patricia Cayo Sexton, Professor, Department of Sociology, New York University, interview, July 16, 1974.

71. Mary Stevenson, "Women's Wages: The Cost of Being Female," a paper presented to the Society for the Study of Social Problems, August 1972, p. 8; cf. Mary Stevenson, *The Determinants of Low Wages for Women Workers*, Ann Arbor, Mich.: Department of Economics, University of Michigan, Ph.D. dissertation, 1974; cf. Barry Bluestone, William M. Murphy, and Mary Stevenson, *Low Wages and the Working Poor*, Ann Arbor, Mich.: The Institute of Labor and Industrial Relations, The University of Michigan, 1973; Barbara R. Bergman, "Prepared Statement: A Policy Agenda for Women's Economic Problems," *in Economic Problems of Women*, hearings pt. 1, July 1973, Washington, D.C.: U.S. Government Printing Office, 1973, pp. 54-58; Robert Bibb, "Blue-Collar Women in Low-Wage Industries: A Dual Labor Market Interpretation," a paper presented at the Annual Meeting of the American Sociological Association, San Francisco, California, August 1975; Elizabeth Waldman and Beverly J. McEaddy, "Where Women Work—An Analysis by Industry and Occupation," *Monthly Labor Review*, vol. 97, May 1974; Dixie Sommers, "Occupational Rankings for Men and Women by Eanings," *Monthly Labor Review*, vol. 97, August 1974.

72. Cf. Dixie Sommers, "Occupational Rankings for Men and Women by Earnings," *Monthly Labor Review*, vol. 97, no. 8, August 1974, tables 1 and 2.

73. Janice Niepert Hedges and Stephen E. Bemis, "Sex Stereotyping: Its Decline in the Skilled Trades," *Monthly Labor Review* 97(5):14, May 1974.

74. Judith Long-Laws, "Causes and Effects of Sex Discrimination in the Bell System," expert witness testimony before the Federal Communications Commission, docket no. 19143, Washington, D.C., 1972, pp. 1-52; reprinted as "The Bell Telephone

System: A Case Study," in Phyllis A. Wallace (ed.), *Equal Employment Opportunity and the A.T. & T. Case*, Cambridge, Mass.: The MIT Press, 1976.

75. Brigid O'Farrell, "Affirmative Action and Skilled Craft Work," Marlboro, Mass.: Learning Center, New England Telephone, stencil; and "Summary: Exploratory Study of Non-Management Women and Work," Marlboro, Mass.: Learning Center, New England Telephone, stencil, 1974.

76. Pamela Roby, "Toward Full Equality: More Job Education for Women," *School Review*, vol 84, no. 2, February 1976; cf. Mary Ellen Verheyden-Hilliard, "Cinderella Doesn't Live Here Anymore," *Manpower*, vol. 7, no. 11, November 1975.

77. In fiscal year 1974, $152.5 million was authorized and $40 million was appropriated for vocational education research and development under the authority of the Vocational Education Amendments of 1968 (P.L. 90-576). These funds are administered by the Bureau of Occupational and Adult Education of the U.S. Office of Education. Additional sums were appropriated for vocational education research and development by the Department of Defense, the Department of Labor, the National Institute of Education, other federal agencies, the states independent of state-administered federal funds, and private foundations. In fiscal year 1974, out of the 93 federally funded projects under Section 131(a), Part C of the Vocational Education Amendments of 1968, only one pertained directly to women (that, directed by Kaufman and Lewis, is described below). U.S. Department of Health, Education, and Welfare, Bureau of Occupational and Adult Education, "Research Projects in Vocational Education: Fiscal Year 1974 Program, Funded Under Section 131(a), Part C, Vocational Education Amendments of 1968, P.L. 90-576," stencil, July 1974. For the distribution of vocational education research funding by other agencies, see Pamela Roby, "Toward Full Equality," op. cit.

78. Interview, Joseph E. Champagne, Principal Investigator, Project on Equal Vocational Education, The Center for Human Resources, University of Houston, March 11, 1974. Cf. Jane Lerner, Fredell Bergstrom, and Joseph E. Champagne, *Equal Vocational Education*, Houston, Texas: The Center for Human Resources, University of Houston. Final report of contracts 52350387 and 62350237 for the Division of Occupational Research and Development, Texas Education Agency, February 1975-June 1976. The project also developed a film, "*All About Eve*," to inform high school sophomores about their need to plan for future careers and about job possibilities for women in traditionally male job areas. The film is available throughout Texas from the Center for Human Resources, University of Houston, Houston, Texas 77004 (713/749-3755).

79. Interview, JoAnn M. Steiger, Steiger, Fink and Smith, Inc., McLean, Virginia, March 17, 1975. The project is funded by the State of Illinois' Office of Vocational Education.

80. Interview, Morgan V. Lewis, Institute for Research on Human Resources, Pennsylvania State University, August 5, 1974. The project is funded under Section 131(a), Part C of the Vocational Education Amendments of 1968 and extends to December 25, 1975; research proposal, "Nontraditional Vocation Education Programs for Women."

81. To date several research agendas have been constructed for the study of sex roles. A few have mentioned the need for research on women in working-class jobs, but none have dealt indepth with what types of research are needed. Cf. Cynthia Fuchs Epstein, "Memo on Research Developments and Needs Pertaining to Changing Sex

Roles," to Dr. Saleen A. Shah, Chief, Center for Studies of Crime and Delinquency, National Institute of Mental Health Research Task Force, 53 pp.; Arlene Kaplan Daniels, "A Survey of Research Concerns on Women's Issues," prepared for RANN, National Science Foundation, stencil, 1973, 63 pp.; published as "Feminist Perspectives in Sociological Research," in Marcia Millman and Rosabeth Moss Kanter (eds.), *Another Voice: Feminist Perspectives on Social Life and Social Science*, New York: Anchor Books, 1975; Hilda Kahne, with Andrew I. Kohen, "Economic Perspectives on the Roles of Women in the American Economy," *Journal of Economic Literature* 13(4):1249-1292, December 1975.

82. Women's Bureau, U.S. Department of Labor, *A Working Woman's Guide To Her Job Rights* (Leaflet 55), Washington, D.C.: U.S. Government Printing Office, 1978.Katherine Stone, *Handbook for OCAW Women*, Denver, Colo.: Oil, Chemical and Atomic Workers International Union, 1973, 82 pp.: cf. U.S. Department of Labor, Women's Bureau, "Brief Highlights of Major Federal Laws and Orders on Sex Discrimination," June 1974, 4 pp.; U.S. Department of Labor, Employment Standards Administration, Wage and Hour Division, "Equal Pay for Equal Work Under the Fair Labor Standards Act," interpretative bull. title 29, part 800 of the Code of Federal Regulations; U.S. Equal Opporutnity Commission, "Guidelines on Discrimination Because of Sex," Washington, D.C.: U.S. Government Printing Office, 1972; and National Commission on the Observance of International Women's Year, *"To Form a More Perfect Union": Justice for American Women*, Washington, D.C.: U.S. Government Printing Office, 1976, pp. 349-362.

83. Cf. U.S. Commission on Civil Rights, *The Federal Civil Rights Enforcement Effort: A Reassessment*, Washington, D.C.: U. S. Government Printing Office, 1973, p. 124; Jerolyn R. Lyle, *Affirmative Action Programs for Women: A Survey of Innovative Programs* (sponsored by the Equal Employment Opportunity Commission and submitted to the Office of Research under contract no. 71-45), Washington, D.C.: U.S. Government Printing Office, 1973; Arvil V. Adams, *Toward Fair Employment and the EEOC: A Study of Compliance Procedures Under Title VII of the Civil Rights Act of 1964* (EEOC contract 70-15 submitted to Research Revision, U.S. Equal Employment Opportunity Commission), Washington, D.C.: U.S. Government Printing Office, 1973.

84. The major equal employment legislation rulings which have been made affecting blue-collar women are a $50 million American Telephone and Telegraph settlement made in January 1973, with the Department of Labor and EEOC; a 1974 consent decree entered between nine steel companies and EEOC, the Department of Labor, and the Department of Justice, involving a backpay award of $30.9 million (2250 to $3,000 per recipient); and the June 1974 Supreme Court ruling affirming that Corning Glass Works award $600,000 in backpay to female workers in the Corning plants.

86. Case no. YCHO-122, decision no. 72-0561, Washington, D.C.: U.S. Equal Employment Opportunity Commission, 1969.

87. The United States Commission on Civil Rights, *The federal Civil Rights Enforcement Effort - 1974*, vol. 1: *To Regulate in the Public Interest*, Washington, D.C.: U.S. Commission on Civil Rights, 1974, pp. ii-iii. The Commission has also published or is publishing relevant reports on equal educational opportunities and on federal civil rights efforts in the areas of employment, federally assisted programs, and policymaking. The Commission's report on employment evaluated the civil

rights activities of most opportunity: the Civil Service Commission, the Department of Labor, the Equal Employment Opportunity Commission, and the Equal Employment Opportunity Coordinating Council. It concluded that "although there has been progress in the last decade, the Federal effort to end employment discrimination based on sex, race, and ethnicity is fundamentally inadequate. It suffers from a number of important deficiencies including lack of overall leadership and direction, the diffusion of responsibility to a number of agencies, the existence of inconsistent policies and standards, the absence of joint investigative or enforcement strategies, and the failure of the agencies covered in this report to develop strong compliance programs." It recommended that "one enforcement agency" be established to apply "one standard of compliance." The United States Commission on Civil Rights, *The Federal Civil Rights Enforcement Effort - 1974*, vol V: *To Eliminate Employment Discrimination*, Washington, D.C.: U.S. Commission on Civil Rights, 1975, p. i. Cf. U.S. Commission on Civil Rights, *The Federal Civil Rights Enforcement Effort - 1974*, vol III: *To Ensure Equal Educational Opportunity*, Washington, D.C.: U.S. Commission on Civil Rights, 1975, and U.S. Commission on Civil Rights, *The Federal Civil Rights Enforcement Effort - 1977: To Eliminate Employment Discrimination: A Sequel*, Washington, D.C.: U.S. Commission on Civil Rights, 1977.

88. "General Accounting Office Finds Federal Enforcement Riddled with Inefficiencies," *Women Today* 5(11):63, May 26, 1975.

89. U.S. General Accounting Office, *The Equal Employment Opportunity Program for Federal Nonconstruction Contractors Can Be Improved*, a report prepared for the use of the Subcommittee on Fiscal Policy of the Joint Economic Committee of the Congress of the United States, Washington, D.C.: U.S. Government Printing Office, 1975, p. iii.

90. "Carter Announces Plans to Reorganize Federal EEO Activities," *Women Today* 8(5):27, March 6, 1978; "EEOC's Norton Outlines Plans for Overhaul of EEOC Functions Before the House," *Women Today* 7(17):103, August 22, 1977.

91. Executive Order 12067 was signed by President Jimmy Carter June 30, 1978; cf. Executive 12107, December 28, 1978; Executive Order 12144, June 22, 1979. *Women Today* 8(5):27.

92. Ibid.

93. *Women Today* 7(17):103.

94. "EEOC Announces New Affirmative Action Guidelines," *Women Today* 7(26): 153, December 26, 1977.

95. Figures for hourly wages, which exclude the effect of part-time and overtime work, support conclusions based on weekly earnings. Elizabeth Waldman and Beverly J. McEaddy, "Where Women Work - An Analysis by Industry and Occupation," *Monthly Labor Review* 97(5): 7, 10, May 1974.

96. Office of the Secretary, U.S. Women's Bureau, "Women in the Labor Force: Annual Averages 1979-1978," ibid., p. 2. In 1970, almost half a million women were working in skilled occupations, up from 277,000 in 1960. The rate of increase (about 80 percent) was twice that for women in all occupations and eight times the rate of increase for men in the skilled trades. Janice Niepert Hedges and Stephen E. Bemis, "Sex Stereotyping: Its Decline in Skilled Trades," *Monthly Labor Review* 97(5):14, May 1974. In May 1974, 524,000 females over age 16 were working in craft and kindred jobs. Cf. Janice Niepert Hedges, "Women Workers and Manpower

Demands in the 1970's," *Monthly Labor Review*, vol. 93, no. 6, June 1970.

97. Jon J. Durkin, "The Potential of Women," research bull. 87, Washington, D.C.: Johnson O'Connor Research Foundation, 1972.

98. "Equal Pay," publ. no. 1320, Wage and Hour Division, Workplace Standards Administration, U.S. Department of Labor, Washington, D.C.: "Interpretative Bulletin: Equal Pay for Equal Work," publ. no. 1209, Wage and Hour Division, Workplace Standards Administration, U.S. Department of Labor, Washington, D.C.

99. Ruth Weyand, Associate General Counsel, International Union of Electrical, Radio and Machine Workers, AFL-CIO, Washington, D.C., interview, January 29, 1974. Cf. Noman D. Willis and Associates, "State of Washington, September 1974," and George Hagglund, "Sex Discrimination: Job Evaluation and Wage Practices Which May Disadvantage Workers," School for Workers, University of Wisconsin — Extension, stencil.

100. In 1974, acting upon the recommendation of the Washington Federation of State Employees and women's organizations, Dan Evans, then governor of the state of Washington, allocated funds for a study to determine whether there are differences in pay between equivalent state jobs filled predominantly (70 percent or more) by one sex. A factor point evaluation system was used in the study, which allowed comparison of unlike jobs. A total of 121 state job classifications were evaluated according to: knowledge and skills required, mental demands, accountability, and working conditions. Norman D. Willis and Associates, who conducted the study, found that "the salaries of jobs predominantly held by women average about 75 percent of the salaries of jobs predominantly held by men. For example, Clerk Typist I and Warehouse Worker I have the same job value (94 points). But the Clerk Typist I field, predominantly female, makes a maximum annual salary of $8,040 while the predominantly male Warehouse Worker I can expect a maximum of $13,104. No women's job made as much as the poorest paid men's job at the same worth. Most women's jobs made less than all men's jobs regardless of worth. For example, Traffic Guide, a predominantly male job, received 89 points; and Licensed Practical Nurse I, predominantly female, received 158 points. Yet the Traffic Guide can expect to earn $11,076 compared to the Licensed Practical Nurse I's earnings of $10,656. Even the Secretary III, predominantly female, at 210 points can expect to earn only $10,800—still less than the Traffic Guide's salary." The gap between "male" and "female" job pay "widens every time there is a pay raise because state salaries are increased on a percentage basis. At the lowest level jobs, the difference between men's and women's rates of pay is $150 per month; at the highest level of responsibility, the difference is about $400 per month." Feminists in the state of Washington are now striving to correct the inequities which the "Comparable Worth," Olympia, Wash.: Washington State Women's Commission (106/753-2870), 1976; and Helen Remick, "Comparable Worth: Equal Pay for Equal Worth," a paper presented at the Annual Meeting of the American Association for Affirmative Action (stencil, Office of Affirmative Action for Women, University of Washington, DW-08, Seattle, Washington 98195), 1977.

101. Mary Witt, Senior Research Analyst, and Patricia Naherny, Research Analyst, Wisconsin Occupational Analysis Field Center, Wisconsin Department of Industry, Labor and Human Relations, Madison, Wisconsin, interview, January 3, 1974. Cf. Mary Witt and Patricia K. Naherny, *Women's Work: Up from .878: Report on D.O.T. Research Project*, Madison, Wis.: University of Wisconsin - Extension, 1975;

Women's Bureau, U.S. Department of Labor, "Research Agenda on the Extent to Which Job and Wage Classification Systems Undervalue Certain Skills and Responsibilities on the Basis of the Sex of the Persons Who Usually Hold the Positions—Discussion Draft," stencil, March, 1979, contact persons: Emilie G. Heller (202) 523-6579; Harriett Harper (202) 523-6601; Jane Walstedt (202) 523-6627.

102. Norma Briggs, a statement read at the First National Working Conference on Women in Blue-Collar Jobs, New York: The Ford Foundation, December 5, 1974.

103. For a very thorough historical, comparative, economic, and social-psychological analysis of the implications of occupational sex segregation, see Martha Blaxall and Barbara B. Reagon (eds.), *Women and the Workplace: The Implications of Occupational Segregation*, Chicago: University of Chicago Press, 1976, also published as *Signs*, vol. 1, no. 3, pt. 2, spring 1976, supplement.

104. Gloria Johnson, Director, Women's Department, International Union of Electrical, Radio and Machine Workers, AFL-CIO, Washington, D.C., interview, February 4, 1974.

105. Herbert H. Meyer and Mary Dean Lee, *The Integration of Females into Traditionally Male-Oriented Jobs: Experiences of Certain Public Utility Companies*, a report prepared for the Employment and Training Administration, U.S. Department of Labor, under research and development contract no. 21-12-75-18, 1976.

106. Cf. Bertrand B. Pogrebin, "Who Shall Work?" *Ms.*, vol. 4, no. 6, December 1975, p. 67; Charlayne Hunter, "Last Hired, and Usually the First Let Go." *New York Times*, January 29, 1975.

107. National Commission on the Observance of International Women's Year, op. cit., p. 60; U.S. Department of Labor, "New Regulations to Help Open Nontraditional Jobs to Women: Consumer Information Leaflet No. USDL—67 (WB-4)," Washington, D.C.: U.S. Government Printing Office, 1978, pp. 1-2. For further information, contact the Office of Federal Contract Compliance Programs, Employment Standards Administration, U.S. Department of Labor, Washington, D.C. 20210.

108. "Sex on the Big Rigs: Women Trucker's Rights Drive," *San Francisco Chronicle*, March 4, 1976. Cf. Lin Farley. *The Sexual Shakedown: The Sexual Harrassment of Women on the Job*, New York: McGraw-Hill, 1978.

109. Stanley Aronowitz, *False Promises: The Shaping of the American Working Class*, New York: McGraw-Hill, 1973, p. 37; cf. Karen Lindsey, "Sexual Harassment on the Job," *Ms.* vol. 6, no. 5, November 1977, pp. 47-48.

110. Research has shown that attitude change often follows policy-induced behavioral changes, as well as that when behavior changes, attitudes matter less. Cf. Robert Coles, *Children of Crisis: A Study of Courage and Fear*, Boston: Little, Brown, 1967.

111. Women's Bureau, U.S. Department of Labor, *Facts About Women's Absenteeism and Labor Force Turnover*, Washington, D.C.: U.S. Government Printing Office, 1969, p. 1.

112. Eula Bingham, *Proceedings: Conference on Women and the Workplace*, June 17-19, 1976, Washington, D.C.: Society for Occupational and Environmental Health (1714 Massachusetts Avenue, N.W., Washington, D.C. 20036; 202/785-8177), 1977. The program included sessions on toxic substances and genetic risks, congenital malformations, and cancer risks to offspring; transplacental cancer from diethylstilbestrol, possible associations between childhood tumors and exposure to chlorinated hydrocarbon pesticides; birth defects and vinyl chloride; psychological

stress factors on families with working women; ergonomic problems associated with certain jobs; occupational disease among beauticians; problems with radiation exposure; women in the textile industry; reproductive effects of lead intoxication; and perspectives on job placement by industry, workers, and Government. Cf. Jeanne H. Stellman, "The Hidden Health Toll: The Cost of Work to the American Woman," *Civil Rights Digest*, vol. 10, no.1, fall 1977; Jeanne M. Stellman, *Women's Work, Women's Health: Myths and Reality*, New York: Pantheon Books, 1977; and Andrea Hricko, *Working for Your Life: A Woman's Guide to Job Health Hazards*, Berkleley, Calif.: Labor Occupational Health Program, University of California, Berkeley, 1976.

113. U.S. Department of Health, Education, and Welfare, *Environmental Health Problems*, Washington, D.C.: Government Printing Office, 1970; Jerome B. Gordon et al., *Industrial Safety Statistics: A Re-examination; A Critical Report Prepared for the Department of Labor*, New York: Praeger Publishers, 1971, both cited in Stellman and Daum, op. cit., pp. 3-4.

114. Jeanne Stellman at the First National Working Conference on Research on Women in Blue-Collar Jobs, New York: the Ford Foundation, December 5, 1974, typed transcript, pp. 187-188; Stellman and Daum, op. cit., pp. xiii-xiv.

115. "The Workplace: Industry's New Question to Women: Your Life or Your Livelihood?," *The Spokeswoman* 7(1):9, 10, July 15, 1976. Cf. Andrea M. Hricko, "Two-Fifths of the Nation's Workforce," *Journal of Social Issues*, vol. 12, no. 2, spring 1975.

116. Myra Wolfgang, International Vice-President and Secretary-Treasurer of Local 705, Hotel and Restaurant Workers Union, Detroit, interview, January 23, 1974.

117. Judy Baston, Assistant Editor, *1199 News*, Local 1199 of the National Union of Hospital and Health Care Employees of the International Union of Retail, Wholesale and Department Store Employees, New York City, interview, February 13, 1974.

118. Vilma R. Hunt, "Occupational Health and the Woman Worker, Working Comments for the First National Working Conference on Research on Women in Blue-Collar Jobs," New York City: The Ford Foundation, December 1974, p. 4. Cf. Vilma R. Hunt, *The Health of Women at Work: A Bibliography*, Evanston, Illinois: The Program on Women, Northwestern University, 1977, 173 pp.

119. Cora Marrett and Andrea Hricko, "Women's Occupational Health: The Rise and Fall of a Research Issue," a paper presented at the American Association for the Advancement of Science Meetings, February 1975.

120. Warren interviewed 766 men and women in eight Detroit area communities in spring 1974 and found that less than 10 percent of both employed and unemployed men, 18 percent of employed women, 23 percent of housewives, and 33 percent of unemployed women reported such stress symptoms as headache, tension, depression, and trouble falling asleep. Other of Warren's findings suggested that the differential number of problems experienced and the differential number of helpers available are reasons which account for the differential amounts of stress. Rachelle Warren, "Stress, Primary Support Systems and the Blue Collar Woman," Ann Arbor, Mich.: Institute of Labor and Industrial Relations, University of Michigan, 1975, stencil, p. 5; Rachelle Warren, "The Work Role and Problem Coping: Sex Differentials in the Use of Helping Systems in Urban Communities," a paper presented at Annual Meeting of the American Sociological Association, San Francisco, August 1975.

121. The *Dictionary of Occupational Titles* (vol. II, U.S. Department of Labor, 1965) has

data on the levels of strength required in various occupations, but sufficient data are not available on the percentage of men and women who can meet these requirements. Hedges and Bemis, op. cit.

122. *The Spokeswoman*, ibid.; Andrea M. Hricko, "Two-Fifths of the Nation's Workforce," *Journal of Current Social Issues*, vol. 12, no. 2, spring 1975; Steve Babson and Nancy Brigham, *What's Happening To Our Jobs?*, Sommerville, Mass.: Popular Economics Press, 1976, pp. 24-26.

123. *The Spokeswoman*, vol. 7, no. 1, op. cit., pp. 7-8.

124. Title VII of the Civil Rights Act, 16004.10. In the United States, the status of pregnancy has been contested in the courts. In September 1975, *The Spokeswoman* reported, "The U.S. Court of Appeals for the Fourth Circuit has joined eight other federal courts in finding that employers who treat pregnancy differently from other temporary disabilities are guilty of sex discrimination in violation of Title VII of the Civil Rights Act. The ruling came in *Gilbert et al. v. General Electric Company*, a class action case filed by G.E. women employees, the International Union of Electrical, Radio and Machine Workers (IUE) and IUE Local 161. The majority opinion in Gilbert generally followed that of the Third Circuit in *Wetzel v. Liberty Mutual Insurance Company*: the court rejected G.E.'s arguments that pregnancy is voluntary and therefore should be excluded from protection and said that the 1974 Supreme Court decision in *Aiollo v. The State of California* did not apply to Title VII cases. The language and intent of Title VII, said the Court, represent 'a flat and absolute prohibition against sex discrimination,' and 'a disability program which, while granting disability benefits generally, denies such benefits expressly for pregnancy . . . is manifestly one which can result in a less comprehensive program of employee compensation and benefits for women employees than for men employees; and would do so on the basis of sex.' The Court also said that whether the employer's policies were intentionally discriminatory is irrelevant because the status looks to 'consequences,' not 'intent'.... Monetary awards to affected employees in the G.E. case are expected to be postponed until the Supreme Court acts on *Wetzel*; G.E. has estimated that losing the case could cost the company $10 million." "G.E. Maternity Case Decided," *The Spokeswoman* 6(3):1, Septemeber 15, 1975. Cf. Joanne L. Levine, "Pregnancy and Sex Based Discrimination in Employment: A Post-Aiollo Analysis," *University of Cincinnati Law Review*, vol. 44, 1975.

125. The case was one of a research technician who became pregnant while working in a hospital laboratory and learned that she was exposed to radiation doses considered safe by the Atomic Energy Commission and OSHA. Her employer could not guarantee, however, that her exposure was safe for her fetus, and asked her either to take unpaid maternity leave or resign. She resigned in order to collect unemployment benefits, but was treated as a new hire when she returned—her seniority and benefits gone and her salary reduced. The EEOC ruled that she was the victim of sex discrimination. The company had violated Title VII, the Commission said, by failing to offer her (a) a transfer to a safe job, (b) the use of maternity and sick leave benefits, or (c) unpaid leave of absence without loss of seniority. *The Spokeswoamn*, vol. 7, no. 1, op. cit., p. 11. In September 1975, 19 states had special provisions limiting the unemployment insurance benefit rights of pregnant women. As a result of legislative action, court decisions, and opinions of attorneys general, this number was down from 38 in August 1971. In states without discriminatory pregnancy

provisions, pregnant women are often discriminated against by unemployment insurance personnel. An excellent summary of unemployment insurance provisions and cases relating to pregnancy is contained in *Manpower* 1(11):30-33, November 1975. For a detailed examination of court and administrative decisions on unemployment insurance for pregnant women, see Unemployment Insurance Service, Manpower Administration, U.S. Department of Labor, *Unemployment Insurance Reports: Supplement on Women*, Benefit Series, Service Report, no. 304, Washington, D.C., 1975.

126. Alice Cook, "Working Mothers Around the World," a colloquium talk sponsored by the Board of Studies in Community Studies, University of California, Santa Cruz, March 1975.

127. Fourteen men who worked at a Virginia plant that manufactured the pesticide kepone are now sterile; lead absorption has been linked to male impotence and abnormal sperm production; children of male operating room attendants have an unusually high incidence of birth defects; and the wives of men exposed to both anesthetic gases and vinyl chloride have unusually high rates of stillbirth and spontaneous abortion. *The Spokeswoman*, vol. 7, no. 1, op. cit., p. 8.

128. One example is the success of the 5-month strike and national boycott by 4,000 refinery workers of the Oil, Chemical and Atomic Workers Union against Shell Oil in 1973. Lead poisoning on the job makes brain damage among oil workers four times more likely than in any other industry, while many refinery workers contract leukemia and other blood diseases from benzene poisoning. The oil companies have failed to test most of the 1,600 chemicals used in refineries. The OCAW struck for a health and safety committee in every plant, the right to call in outside inspectors approved by the union, access to previously confidential information on chemicals used in the refineries, and company-financed annual medical checkups for all workers. Babson and Brigham, op. cit., p. 26.

129. Alice H. Cook, memo to Urban Institute Conference on Priorities for Research on Women, Washington, D.C., June 18, 1974.

130. "California's Protective Laws Endangered," *The Spokeswoman* 4:4, May 14, 1974. In a 1974 ruling, instead of extending the requirement of overtime pay after 8 hours of work per day to men, the California State Industrial Welfare Commission voted to require overtime pay only after 10 hours of work per day for all employees, to eliminate scheduled rest periods and lounges, and to allow mandatory 10-hour working days. Between 1969 and 1973, 15 states repealed their maximum hours laws for women. In others, federal courts and a state supreme court have held that the state hours laws conflict with Title VII; a few have held tht women *may* work beyond the maximum hours limitations but *may not* be required to do so. Only Nevada continues to enforce a law setting 12 hours per day and 56 hours per week as absolute maximums for women and requiring overtime pay after 8 hours per day and 48 hours per week. Cf. *Union Labor Report, Weekly Newsletter*, Bureau of National Affairs, June 20, 1974; Women's Bureau, U.S. Department of Labor, "State Hours Laws for Women: Changes in Status Since the Civil Rights Act of 91964," Washington, D.C.: U.S. Government Printing Office, 1974 (revised).

131. Cf. Riva Poor (ed.), *4 Days, 40 Hours: Reporting a Revolution in Work and Leisure*, Cambridge: Bursk and Poor, 1970; Ellen B. Hoffman, "The Four-Day Week Raises New Problems," *The Conference Board Record* 9:21-25, February 1972; Janice Niepert Hedges, "New Patterns for Working Time," *Monthly Labor Review*, vol. 96,

no. 2, February 1973; *Directory on Alternative Work Patterns* published by the National Council for Alternative Work Patterns, Gail Rosenberg, President, (1925 K Street, NW., Washington, D.C. 20006; 202/466-4467).

132. Anne Nelson at the First National Working Conference on Research on Women in Blue-Collar Jobs, New York: The Ford Foundation, December 5, 1974, typed transcript, pp. 82-83.

133. Bureau of Labor Statistics, U.S. Department of Labor, "BLS Revises Estimates for Urban Family Budget and Comparative Indexes for Selected Urban Areas," press release, USDL 76-759, May 5, 1976.

134. Bureau of Economic Analysis, U.S. Department of Commerce, *Local Area Personal Income 1969-1974*, vol. 1, Summary, PB 254-055, June 1976, table 1.

135. For very preliminary work in this area, see Pamela Roby, "Shared Parenting: Perspectives from Other Nations," *School Reviews*, vol. 83, no. 3, May 1975; Katherine Walker, "Time Budget Research on Working Women,' Ithaca, N.Y.: Department of Consumer Economics and Public Policy, Cornell University, stencil; Kathryn E. Walker and William H. Guager, "The Dollar Value of Houshold Work," bull. 60, New York State College of Human Economy (available for 25 cents from the Mailing Room, Research Park, Cornell University, Ithaca, New York 14850).

136. Cf. Roby, ibid.; Carolyn Shaw Bell, "Alternatives for Social Change: The Future Status of Women," a paper prepared for the Mr. and Mrs. Spencer T. Olin Conference on the Status of Women in Higher Education and the Professions, Washington University, St. Louis, Missouri, April 1975.

137. Carol S. Greenwald, "Part-Time Work and Flexible Hours Eployment," a paper presented to Workshop on Research Needed to Improve the Employment and Employability of Women, U.S. Department of Labor, Washington, D.C.: *Statistics 1973*, table 21, and *Employment and Earnings*, vol. 21, no. 7, January 1975, table A-7, p. 27; Office of the Secretary, U.S. Women's Bureau, "Women in the Labor Force: Annual Averages 1979-1978." op. cit., p. 2.

138. Anne Nelson, Associate Director, Trade Union Women's Studies Program, New York State School of Industrial and Labor Relations, Cornell University, at the First National Working Conference on Research on Women in Blue-Collar Jobs, New York: The Ford Foundation, December 5, 1974, typed transcript, p. 89.

139. Cf. Erik Gronseth, "Work-Sharing Families: Husband-Wife Both in Part-Time Employment," Institute of Sociology, Oslo University, paper presented at the Gottlieb Duttweiler Institute, Ruschlikon by Zurich, June 1972; Pamela A. Roby, "Shared Parenting: Perspectives from Other Nations," *School Review*, vol. 83, no. 3, May 1975; Carolyn Shaw Bell, "Alternatives for Social Change: The Future Status of Women," Department of Economics, Wellesley College, Working Paper no. 14, 1975.

140. William H. Chafe, *The American Woman: Her Changing Social, Economic, and Political Roles, 1920-1970*, New York: Oxford University Press, 1975, p. 185.

141. Barry Bluestone, The Tripartite Economy. Labor Markets and the Working Poor," *Poverty and Human Resources* 5(4):15-35.

142. For a detailed analysis of the data that are available and the data that are needed on the employment status of minority-group women, see Patricia Cayo Sexton, "Minority Group Women," a paper prepared for the workshop on Research Needed to Improve the Employment and Employability of Women, Women's Bureau, U.S. Department of Labor, Washington, D.C., June 1974. Cf. Phyllis A. Wallace,

Pathways to Work: Unemployment Among Black Teenage Females, Lexington, Mass.: Lexington Books, 1974; Women's Bureau, U.S. Department of Labor, "Facts on Women Workers of Minority Races," Washington, D.C.: U.S. Government Printing Office, 1974.

143. Bureau of Labor Statistics, U.S. Department of Labor, *Employment and Earnings*, vol. 27, no. 1, January 1980, p. 166.

144. Ibid., p. 159. Minority women sixteen years and older had an overall unemployment rate of 14 percent in 1975.

145. Bureau of Labor Statistics, U.S. Department of Labor, *Special Labor Force Report*, July 1975, p. 1.

146. Bureau of Labor Statistics, U.S. Department of Labor, *Employment and Earnings*, vol. 22, no. 7, January 1976, annual averages, table 1; vol. 25, no. 1, January 1978, p. 137.

147. Cf. John C. Leggett and Claudette Cervinka, "Countdown: Labor Statistics Revisited," *Society* 10(1):99-103, November/December 1972.

148. Bertram Gross and Stanley Moses, "Measuring the Real Work Force: 25 Million Unemployed," *Social Policy* 3(3):10, September/October 1972.

149. Marilyn Bender, "Job Discrimination, 10 Years Later," *New York Times*, November 10, 1974; Seymour L. Wolfbein, Dean, School of Business Administration, Temple University, and former Director of the Office of Manpower, Automation and Training, U.S. Department of Labor, quoted in *Women Today* 4(25):158, December 9, 1974; Bernice Sandler, Director of the Project on the Status and Education of Women, Association of American Colleges, quoted in *Women Today* 4(16):168, December 23, 1974.

150. Gloria Johnson at the First National Working Conference on Research on Women in Blue-Collar Jobs, New York: The Ford Foundation, December 5, 1974, typed transcript, p. 107.

151. Cf. Alfred W. Blumrosen and Ruth G. Blumrosen, "Layoff or Work Sharing: The Civil Rights Act of 1974 in the Recession of 1975," *The Civil Rights Digest*, vol. 7, no. 3, spring 1975; Bertrand B. Pogrebin, "Who Shall Work?," *Ms.*, vol. 4, no. 6, December 1975, p. 67.

152. "CLUR Hits NOW Seniority Stand," *CLUW News* 1(2):3, summer 1975.

153. "Union Seniority Clauses Termed Safeguard for Women, Minorities," ibid., p. 1.

154. "AFL-CIO Policy Statement Says Congress Should Act to Cut Unemployment to 3%," *Wall Street Journal*, December 8, 1975, p. 1.

155. The National Organization for Women has recommended to Congress that such an act should have a specific commitment to developing new, supplementary training and counseling programs for women about opportunities in nontraditional jobs; include "Equal Opportunity" in its title as a declaration of congressional intent to not only provide employment but to assure equity as well; use a 37 percent rate of unemployment only as an interim goal and define it as a goal for *each* labor force group—women, minorities, youth, older persons, etc.; give special consideration to the employment problems of these groups; reestablish the concept of "job guarantee" for any person who wishes to work; prohibit forcing people off income maintenance into work neither feasible nor desirbale for them; and have social service rather than military be priority programs. Elaine Day Latourell, "Legislative Report," *Do It Now* 9(6):12, July 1976.

For background reading on the question of full employment, see "Women and Full Employment," Women's Equity Action League, *Washington Report*, vol. 5, no. 4, October 1976; Gloria Steinem, "A Coalition for Full Employment," *Social Policy*, vol. 5, no. 3, September 1974; Bertram Gross, "Reconsidering Unemployment," and editorial, "Jobs for Whom? to Do What?," both in *Social Policy*, vol. 5, no. 5, January 1975; Howard M. Wachtel, "Looking at Poverty from Radical, Conservative, and Liberal Perspectives," *in* Pamela Roby (ed.), *The Poverty Establishment*, Englewood Cliffs, N.J.: Prentice-Hall, Inc., 1974; David Gordon, *Theories of Poverty and Underemployment*, Lexington, Mass.: Heath-Lexington Books, 1973; Sar A. Levitan, "Does Public Job Creation Offer Any Hope?," *The Conference Board Record*, vol. XII, no. 8, August 1975; Robert Lekachman, "Breaking the Phillips Curve: Yes We Can Afford Full Employment," *The New Leader*, July 21, 1975; Moses Lukaczer, "The Idea of Full Employment," and Ruth Jordan, "Full Employment—A Women's Issue?," *Civil Rights Digest*, vol. 8, no. 2-3, winter-spring 1976; *Employment Problems of Women, Minorities and Youth*, hearings before the Subcommittee on Economic Growth of the Joint Economic Committee, 94th Congress of the United States, Washington, D.C.: U.S. Government Printing Office, July 7 and 8, 1975; Leon H. Keyserling, "The Social Costs of Unemployment," testimony before the Joint Economic Committee, 94th Congress of the United States, February 16, 1976.

156. The latest version of the Humphrey-Hawkins bill (H.R. 50) aims to reduce overall unemployment to 4 percent within five years but does not mandate how the government is to achieve that goal. *Manpower and Vocational Education Weekly* 8(46):1, November 17, 1977.

157. Chela Sandoval, University of California - Santa Cruz student, conversation, June 3, 1974.

158. Alexis Herman, Director, Black Woman's Employment Program, Atlanta, Georgia, at the First National Working Conference on Research on Women in Blue-Collar Jobs, New York: The Ford Foundation, December 6, 1974, typed transcript.

159. Cf. Howard M. Wachtel, "Looking at Poverty from Radical, Conservative, and Liberal Perspectives," *in* Pamela Roby (ed.), *The Poverty Establishment*, Englewood Cliffs, N.J.: Prentice-Hall, 1974; S.M. Miller and Pamela Roby, *The Future of Inequality*, New York: Basic Books, 1970, ch. 6.

160. Title IX of the 1972 U.S. Education Amendments states: "No persons in the United States shall, on the basis of sex, be excluded from participating in, be denied the benefits of or be subjected to discrimination under any educational program or excluded from actively receiving federal financial assistance...." Title I, "Prohibition of Sex Discrimination," U.S. Education Amendments of 1972, P.L. 92-318, 92d Congress, S. 659, June 23, 1972. For a description of the status of women in military training programs, see Carol C. Parr, "Testimony Before the Subcommittee on Priorities and Economy in Government of the Joint Economic Committee of the U.S. Congress Concerning Women in the Military, September 1, 1977," National Coalition for Women in Defense, 733 15th St., N.W., Suite 200, Washington, D.C. 20005; and Martin Binkin and Shirley J. Bach, *Women and the Military*, Washington, D.C.: The Brookings Institution, 1977.

161. Manpower Administration, U.S. Department of Labor, *Women in Apprenticeship— Why Not?*, Manpower Research Monograph no. 33, Washington, D.C.: U.S. Government Printing Office, 1974, p. 1. Nationwide, at least a small number of

women were in 106 of the 350 apprenticeable trades (U.S. Department of Labor, Women's Bureau, "Nontraditional Occupations for Women," Washington, D.C., December 1973, stencil). Cf. Norma Briggs, "Women Apprentices: Removing the Barriers," *Manpower* 6(12):3-11, December 1974.

162. Ibid., pp. 1-2.

163. Ibid., p. 13.

164. Ibid., p. 16.

165. These percentages include homemaking, which does not fall within the definition of vocational education used above and by the U.S. Congress. Despite the congressional definition, most vocational education data provided by the U.S. Office of Education include homemaking, which is not "preparation for gainful employment" (data calculated from Bureau of Adult, Vocational and Technical Education, *Summary Data: Vocational Education, Fiscal Year 1972*, Washington, D.C.: Office of Education, U.S. Department of Health, Education, and Welfare, May 1973, p. 2).

166. Ibid., pp. 2, 14-17; and U.S. Department of Labor, Women's Bureau, "Issues in Vocational Training for Women and Girls," Washington, D.C., stencil, December 1973. Vocational education is composed of the following major program areas: agriculture, distribution, health, home economics (gainful), office, technical, trades and industry, and special programs. Among the 19 major instructional programs included in the "distribution" area are advertising services, apparel and accessories, automotive, finance and credit, floristry, and food distribution. Dental assistant, medical lab assistant, practical nurse, and physical therapist are among the instructional programs in the health area. Gainful home economics includes care and guidance of children and food management service. The office area includes accounting and computing, filing and office machines, and stenography, secretarial, and typing programs. Among the 21 major instructional programs in the technical area are aeronautical, architectural, automotive, chemical, electrical, and metallurgical technology. Among the 44 major instructional programs in the trade and industrial area are air conditioning, appliance repair, auto mechanics, blueprint reading, business machines maintenance, carpentry, electricity, masonry, plumbing and pipefitting, drafting, graphic arts, cosmetology, and textile production (Leonard A. Lecht, "Priorities in Vocational Education: Recent Developments and Potentials for Change During the 1970's," *Looking Ahead* 20(7):1, November 1972; see Kaufman et al., pp. 5-36.

167. Cf. Mary L. Ellis, "Women in Technical Education," *Technical Education News* 31(2):5-6, April 1972; Ellis, "Let's Examine Emerging Changes in the Labor Force and Adjust Our Educational Programs for Women's Role as Workers," *Industrial Education*, December 1972, p. 80.

168. Cf. Rupert N. Evans, Garth L. Mangum, and Otto Pragan, *Education for Employment: The Background and Potential of the 1968 Vocational Education Amendments*, Ann Arbor: University of Michigan, Institute of Labor and Industrial Relations, 1969; Jacob J. Kaufman, Carl J. Schaefer, Morgan V. Lewis, David W. Stevens, and Elaine W. House, *The Role of Secondary Schools in the Preparation of Youth for Employment: A Comparative Study of the Vocational, Academic, and General Curricula*, University Park, Pa.: Institute for Research on Human Resources, The Pennsylvania State University, 1967.

169. Kaufman et al. found in a study of 1,070 male and 856 female vocational education

graduates from six cities of varying size that 23 percent of both men and women graduates obtained their first job through school placement, but 16 percent of the males as compared with only 19 percent of the females obtained their first jobs through personal or family friends, and 13 percent of the females as compared with only 7 percent of the males obtained their first jobs through public or private employment agencies. Most males (34 percent) and females (31 percent) obtained their first jobs by direct application. Kaufman, ibid., table 6.15, p. 6-21.

170. See Dixie Sommers, "Occupational Rankings for Men and Women by Earnings, *Monthly Labor Review*, vol. 97, no. 8, August 1974, tables 1 and 2.

171. Janice Niepert Hedges and Stephen E. Bemis, op. cit., p. 14.

172. Congress authorized $152.5 million or nearly four times as much as was appropriated for vocational education research and development for fiscal year 1974.

173. Monica K. Sinding (Research Associate, Committee on Vocational Education Research and Development, Assembly of Behavioral and Social Sciences, National Research Council) reports receipt of several letters from government officials indicating that they have no knowledge of plans for research in "how vocational education might be adjusted to better meet the needs of girls and women" (letters from Ralph R. Canter, Program Manager, Life Sciences Directorate, Air Force Office of Scientific Research, U.S. Department of the Air Force; Glenn C. Boerrighter, Chief, Research Branch, Division of Research and Demonstration, Office of Education, September 16, 1974; Howard Rosen, Director, Office of Manpower Research and Development, Manpower Administration, U.S. Department of Labor). The Division of Manpower Development and Training of the U.S. Office of Education in 1974 noted that "over 90 percent" of the female trainees in MDTA institutional programs "have been enrolled in either clerical, food services, or health related occupational training" and that although "the income level of both men and women increases after MDTA training, ...the income level of women *after* training has never reached the pre-training income level of men" (U.S. Department of Health, Education, and Welfare, Government Contracting Office, Office of Education, "New Careers for Women," mimeographed, Washington, D.C.: U.S. Department of Health, Education, and Welfare, 1974).

174. U.S. Department of Health, Education, and Welfare, Bureau of Occupational and Adult Education, "Research Projects in Vocational Education: Fiscal Year 1974 Program, Funded Under Section 131 (a), Part C, Vocational Education Amendments of 1968 P.L. 90-576," mimeographed, Washington, D.C.: U.S. Department of Health, Education, and Welfare, 1974.

175. Kathryn L. Mulligan, "A Question of Opportunity: Women and Continuing Education," Washington, D.C.: National Advisory Council on Extension and Continuing Education, March 1973, p. 25.

176. Interview, Mary Wingrove, Curriculum Development Branch, Bureau of Occupational and Adult Education, U.S. Department of Health, Education, and Welfare, August 12, 1974; interview, Dr. Joyce Cook, Acting Chief, Demonstration Branch, Bureau of Occupational and Adult Education, U.S. Department of Health, Education, and Welfare, August 16, 1974.

177. The State of Illinois Office of Vocational Education in 1974 allocated $30,000 to JoAnn M. Steiger of Steiger, Fink and Smith, Inc., McLean, Va., for curriculum materials to encourage girls to consider a wider range of jobs. The same year, the New Hampshire Office of Vocational Education used Part C monies to fund

instructional materials geared to women on "Careers in Building Trades" (Langdon Plumer, Director of Vocational Education, Exeter High School, Exeter, N.H., letter to Pamela Roby, November 4, 1974). The Division of Occupational Research and Development of the Texas Education Agency has used Part C monies to develop means to recruit women into vocation programs traditionally dominated by men ("Equal Vocational Education," a project by the Center for Human Resources, University of Houston, in cooperation with the Houston Independent School District, sponsored by the Division of Occupational Research and Development, Texas Education Agency, February 1975-June 1976, mimeographed, Houston, Texas: University of Houston, p.3).

178. "Wanted: Anyone Hurt by Sex Bias in Vocational Training," *Civil Liberties*, June 1976, p. 3; *How to Erase Sex Discrimination in Vocational Education*, Literature Clerk, American Civil Liberties Union, 22 East 40th Street, New York, New York 10016 ($2.50). Cf. Project on Equal Education Rights, *Stalled at the Start: Government on Equal Education Rights*, NOW Legal Defense and Education Fund, 1977.

179. *Sex Discrimination and Sex Stereotyping in Vocational Education*, hearings before the Subcommittee on Elementary, Secondary, and Vocational Education of the Committee on Education and Labor, House of Representatives, 94th Congress, 1st sess., 1975, Washington, D.C.: U.S. Government Printing Office, 1975.

180. S. 2603, "Women's Vocational Education Amendments of 1975."

181. "Washington Report," *The Spokeswoman* 7(5):7, November 15, 1976.

182. Norma Briggs, "Apprenticeship," Joint Economic Committee of the Congress of the United States, *American Women Workers in a Full Employment Economy*, September 15, 1977, 95th Congress, 1st sess., p. 225.

183. During fall 1976, posters showing women in nontraditional jobs were displayed prominently in the lobby of the Employment and Training Office Building. Cf. the November 1975 issue of *Manpower* entitled *Womanpower*, particularly Edwin Harris, "In the Manner of Rosie the Riveter," *Womanpower* 7(11):26-29, November 1975.

184. *Women Today* 6(9):61, April 26, 1976.

185. Manpower Administration, *Women in Apprenticeship*, op. cit., p. 3; in April 1974, the Manpower Administration amended three of its Apprenticeship Outreach contracts to provide new opportunities for women. The Apprenticeship Outreach Program, since its inception in 1964, has been directed toward recruiting minority men into apprentice trades. The expanded program places special emphasis on recruiting young women, who are given the necessary counseling and tutoring to prepare them to enter all apprenticeable occupations. Three organizations operate pilot projects in six selected cities. The National Urban league expanded its programs in Atlanta, Chicago, and Los Angeles. The Mexican-American Foundation will conduct a second outreach program in Los Angeles. The Recruitment and Training Program, Inc., formerly the Workers Defense League of the A. Philip Randolph Foundation, will expand its programs in Boston, Cleveland, and New York. Women's Bureau, U.S. Department of Labor, "Steps to Opening the Skilled Trades," June 1974, p. 7. Better Jobs for Women in Denver, which is funded under CETA (Comprehensive Employment and Training Act), and San Francisco's Women in Apprenticeship are other new apprenticeship outreach programs for women. B. Kimball Baker, "How to Succeed in a Journeyman's World," *Manpower* 7(11):38-42, November 1975.

186. Joan Slowitsky, "Occupation Outlook Handbook in Brief," 1974-75 ed., *Occupational Outlook Quarterly*, vol. 18, no. 2, summer 1974. Between 1960 and 1973, the number of women employed as craft workers increased from 277,140 to 561,000. Women's Bureau, "Steps to Opening the Skilled Trades," op. cit., p. 1; U.S. Department of Labor, "New Regulations to Help Open Nontraditional Jobs to Women—Consumer Information Leaflet USDL-67 (WB-4)," op. cit.. For further information contact the Bureau of Apprenticeship and Training, Employment and Training Administration, U.S. Department of Labor, Washington, D.C. 20213.

187. Norma Briggs, interview, op. cit.

188. *Women in Apprenticeship—Why Not?*, op. cit., p. 18.

189. Seifer, op. cit., p. 67.

190. Barbara Wertheimer and Anne Nelson, "Into the Mainstream: Equal Educational Opportunity for Working Women," *Journal of Research and Development in Education*, vol. 10, no. 4, 1977.

191. Herbert E. Striner, *Continuing Education as a National Capital Investment*, Washington D.C.: W.E. Upjohn Institute for Employment Research, 1972; Striner, "Recurrent Education and Manpower Training in Great Britain," *Monthly Labor Review* 98(9):30-34, September 1975.

192. Alice Cook, Professor Emeritus, New York State School of Industrial and Labor Relations, Cornell University, at the First National Working Conference on Research on Women in Blue-Collar Jobs, New York: The Ford Foundation, December 6, 1974, typed transcript, pp. 50-52.

193. Cf. Sally Hillsman Baker, "Women in Blue-Collar and Service Occupations," *in* A. Yates and S. Harkess (eds.), *Women and Their Work*, Palo Alto, Calif.: Mayfield Publishing Co., in press.

194. Barry Bluestone, William M. Murphy, and Mary Stevenson, *Low Wages and the Working Poor*, Ann Arbor, Mich.: The Institute of Labor and Industrial Relations, 1973, pp. 28-31; cf. Robert T. Averitt, *The Dual Economy: The Dynamics of American Industry Structure*, New York: W.W. Norton and Co., 1968; Louis A. Ferman, "The Irregular Economy," Institute of Labor and Industrial Relations, mimeograph, 1969.

195. Women's Bureau, U.S. Department of Labor, *1975 Handbook on Women Workers*, op. cit., table 45, p. 115.

196. Barry Bluestone, "Labor Markets, Defense Subsidies and the Working Poor," *in* Pamela Roby (ed.), *The Poverty Establishment*, op. cit., pp. 209-210.

197. Wage and Hour Division, U.S. Department of Labor, *Handy Reference Guide to the Fair Labor Standards Act*, Washington, D.C.: U.S. Government Printing Office, 1977.

198. National Commission on the Observance of International Women's Year, "*To Form a More Perfect Union": Justice for American Women*, op. cit., pp. 55-56.

199. Women's Bureau, U.S. Department of Labor, "Ban Against Pregnancy Discrimination," Washington D.C.: U.S. Department of Labor, March 1979, 2 pages.

200. The new law overturned the U.S. Supreme Court rulings that employers need *not* compensate women for maternity-related disability on the same basis as they compensate employees for other disabilities (*General Electric v. Gilbert et al.*, December 7, 1976 and *Nashville Gas Company v. Satty*, December 6, 1977).

201. U.S. Supreme Court, *Nashville Gas Company v. Satty*. December 6, 1977.

202. Cf. Susan Ferge, "The Development of the Protection of Mothers and Children in Hungary After 1945," and Rivka Bar-Yosef Weiss, "Pre-School Child Care in Israel,"

in Pamela Roby (ed.), *Child-Care—Who Cares? Foreign and Domestic Infant and Early Childhood Development Policies,* New York: Basic Books, 1973.

203. Women's Bureau, "Ban Against Pregnancy Discrimination," op. cit., p.1.

204. "Abortion," *Alert,* December 1977, p. 2.

205. Spencer Rich, "New Curbs Cut Medicaid-Funded Abortions 99%, HEW Reports," *The Washington Post,* March 8, 1979.

206. Marcie Greenstein, "Abortion Bill Out," *Women's Political Times* 2(4):4, winter 1977.

207. Linda Tarr-Whelan, Deputy Director of Program Development, AFSCME, interview, February 1, 1974.

208. Jennifer Gerner, *Wisconsin Maternity Leave and Fringe Benefits: Policies, Practices, and Problems,* report to the Manpower Administration, U.S. Department of Labor, grant 21-55-73-22, fiscal year 1975.

209. Cf. Deborah A. Lewis, "Insuring Women's Health," *Social Policy* 2(1):19-25, May/June 1976.

210. U.S. Civil Rights Commission, *Women and Poverty,* Washington, D.C.: U.S. Civil Rights Commission, 1974, p. 42.

211. Elizabeth Waldman and Robert Whitmore, "Children of Working Mothers, March 1973," *Monthly Labor Review* 97(5):53, May 1974, table 2; Allyson Sherman Grossman, "Children of Working Mothers, March 1976," *Monthly Labor Review* 100(76):42, table 1.

212. Mary Dublin Keyserling, *Window on Day Care: A Report on the Findings of the National Council on Jewish Women,* New York: National Council of Jewish Women, 1974.

213. Cf. *A Union Sponsored Day Center,* New York: Amalgamated Clothing Workers Union, 1972; *The Union and the Day Care Center,* New York: Amalgamated Clothing Workers Union, 1972. For a discussion of employer-provided childcare, see Susan Stein, "The Company Cares for Children," *in* Pamela Roby (ed.), *Child Care—Who Cares? Foreign and Domestic Infant and Early Childhood Development Policies,* New York: Basic Books, Inc., 1973.

214. For further analysis of childcare policies and proposals, see Pamela Roby (ed.), *Child Care—Who Cares?,* op. cit.

215. Joyce D. Miller, "The Urgency of Child Care," *AFL-CIO American Federationist,* vol. 82, June 1975.

216. Alice H. Cook, Professor Emeritus, Industrial and Labor Relations, Cornell University, interview, February 15, 1974.

217. Roby (ed.) *Child Care—Who Cares?,* op. cit., pp. 306-309.

218. Laura Perlman, op. cit., p. 32.

219. Arlie Hochschild has studied and empathetically reported on one small community, an apartment house of rural-born, working-class, white, Anglo-Saxon Protestant widowed females in their late sixties. Many of the old women in this San Francisco community had been employed in such places as factories, laundries, and lunch counters. They lived on welfare, Social Security, and/or pensions. Arlie Russell Hochschild, *The Unexpected Community,* Englewood Cliffs, N.J.: Prentice-Hall, Inc., 1973.

220. U.S. Commission on Civil Rights, *Women and Poverty,* Washington, D.C.: U.S. Commission on Civil Rights, June 1974, p. 43; U.S. Department of Health, Education, and Welfare, U.S. Labor Department, and U.S. Treasury Department, *Coverage and Vesting of Full-Time Employees Under Private Retirement Plans,* April 1972.

221. Martha W. Griffiths, "Can We Still Afford Occupational Segregation? Some Remarks," *Signs* 1(3):12.

222. In 1972, approximately 140 million persons had some earnings credited under the Social Security system and about 51 million persons were working under some type of employer-employee retirement plan (ibid., p. 42).

223. Nancy Seifer, "Statement Submitted to the New York Senate, Committee on the Judiciary, Hearings on the Equal Rights Amendment," New York: Institute on Pluralism and Group Identity, American Jewish Committee, March 11, 1975, p. 6. Cf. Lenore Weiss, "Social Security: women Who Fall Betwen the Cracks," Union WAGE, no. 27, January 1975, p. 8; Lenore Bixby, "Woman and Social Security" Social Security Bulletin, vol. 35, September 1972; Lucy B. Mallan, "Women Born in the Early 1900's: Employment Earnings and Benefit Levels," *Social Security Bulletin*, vol. 37, March 1974; Martha Griffiths, "Sex Discrimination in Income Security Programs," *Notre Dame Lawyer*, vol. 49, February 1974.

224. Joe A. Miller and Louis A. Ferman, "Welfare Careers and Low Wage Employment," report prepared for the Manpower Administration, U.S. Department of Labor, under contract no. 51-24-69-05, December 1972, pp. 91-97.

225. For an organizational analysis of the processes through which the very institutions that are nominally intended to include the excluded bar the excluded, see S.M. Miller, Pamela Roby, and Alwine A. de Vos van Steewijk, "Creaming the Poor," *Trans-action* 7(8):38-43, June 1970.

226. Cf. Joseph Giordano, *Ethnicity and Mental Health: Research and Recommendations*, New York: American Jewish Committee, 1973.

227. Cf. The Boston Women's Health Book Collective, *Our Bodies, Ourselves*, New York: Simon and Schuster, 1971; Ellen Frankfort, *Vaginal Politics*, New York: Quadrangle, 1972.

228. Much relevant literature has been reviewed on low-income and blue-collar health patterns in S.M. Miller and Pamela Roby, *The Future of Inequality*, op. cit.

229. The survey was administered in 1966 to a national probability sample of the noninstitutional civilian population of women aged 30 to 44. Parnes et al., *Dual Careers: A Longitudinal Study of Labor Market Experience of Women*, vol. 1, Washington, D.C.: Manpower Administration, U.S. Department of Labor, 1975, p. 119. Cf. Harold Feldman and Margaret Feldman, *A Study of the Effects on the Family Due to Employment of the Welfare Mother*, report prepared for the Manpower Administration, U.S. Department of Labor, under research contract no. 51-34-69-07, 1972, pp. 177-283; and Parnes et al., *Dual Careers: A Longitudinal Analysis of the Labor Market Experience of Women*, vol. 4, Washington, D.C.: Manpower Administration, U.S. Department of Labor, 1975, pp. 18-19. Cf. Jane Roberts Chapman, "Sex Discrimination in Credit: The Backlash of Economic Dependency," *in* Jane Roberts Chapman (ed.), op. cit.

230. Patricia and Brendon Sexton, *Blue-Collars and Hard Hats*, New York: Random House, 1971.

231. Myra Komarovsky, *Blue-Collar Marriage*, New York: Random House, 1964.

232. Harold Sheppard and Neal Q. Herrick, *Where Have All the Robots Gone?*, New York: The Free Press, 1972. Also see Richard Sennett and Jonathan Cobb, *The Hidden Injuries of Class*, New York: Alfred A. Knopf, 1972.

233. Ruth Weyand, Associate General Counsel, International Union of Electrical Workers, Washington, D.C., interview, January 29, 1974.

234. Rose Board, member of U.A.W. Local 400, President of U.A.W. Women's Committee, Regions 1, 1A, 1B, and 1I, Detroit, interview, January 20, 1974.

235. William Ryan, *Blaming the Victim*, New York: Random House, 1971.

236. Judith Long-Laws, op. cit.

237. Gloria Johnson, Director, Women's Department, Social Action Division, International Union of Electrical Workers, Washington, D.C., interview, February 4, 1974.

238. Kathy McCourt, Research Sociologist, National Opinion Research Center, Chicago, interview, January 10, 1974.

239. Many women's support groups are part of or have grown out of reevaluation counseling or co-counseling. for further information, see *Sisters*, nos. 1,2,3, and 4; *Black Re-emergency*, nos. 1 and 2; and *Working for a Living*, nos. 1 and 2, all published by Rational Island Publishers, 719 Second Avenue North, Seattle, Washington 98109; and Harvey Jackins, *The Human Side of Human Beings: The Theory of Re-evaluation Counseling*, Seattle: Rational Island Publishers, 1965. For a description of consciousness-raising techniques, see Pamela Allen, *Free Space*, Washington, N.J.: Times Change Press, 1971.

240. Seifer, op. cit., pp. 66-67.

241. Ibid., pp. 78-79.

242. "1980 Broadcast Awards," National Commission on Women and Work, 1200 Connecticut Avenue, NW/suite 310, Washington, D.C. 20036.

243. "Women Civilian Labor Force Partcipation and Union and Association Membership in the United States, 1952-76," U.S. Department of Labor, Bureau of Labor Statistics, June 1976.

244. "Women Members in Unions and Associations with 50,000 Women Members or More in 1972, and Earlier Selected Years," U.S. Department of Labor, Bureau of Labor Statistics, Division of Industrial Relations, June 1974.

245. Alice Cook, interview, op. cit. For a foundation on union organizing, read Stephen I. Schlossberg and Fredrick E. Sherman, *Organizing and the Law: A Handbook for Union Organizers*, Washington, D.C: The Bureau of National Affairs, Inc., 1971; and Union WAGE, *Organize! A Working Women's Handbook; Working Women and Their Organizations—150 Years of Struggle; Women in the Labr Movement*, all available from Union WAGE, P.O. Box 462, Berkeley, California 94701.

246. "Women's Groups and Labor Movement Work Toegether for Labor Reform," *Women Today* 7(19):118, 1977.

247. "Resolutions Adopted by Delegates to the National Women's Conference," *Women Today* 7(24):5, December 12, 1977.

248. Bureau of Labor Statistics, U.S. Department of Labor, *Directory of National Unions and Employee Associations, 1975*, Washington, D.C.: U.S. Government Printing Office, 1977, p. 66; cf. Virginia A. Bergquist, "Women's Participation in Labor Organizations," *Monthly Labor Review*, vol. 97, no. 10, October, 1974; Gail Falk, "Sex Discrimination in the Trade Unions: Legal Resources for Change," *in* Jo Freeman (ed.), *Women: A Feminist Perspective*, Palo Alto, Calif.: Mayfield Press, 1975, pp. 254-276.

249. William J. Eaton, "Women Seeking Union Clout," *Philadelphia Inquirer*, December 13, 1977.

250. Mim Kelber, "A.F.L.-C.I.O. - For Men Only?," *The Nation*, November 17, 1979, p. 491.

251. Ibid.

252. Ibid., p. 492.

253. Gloria Johnson, op. cit.

254. Only men addressed the 1977 AFL-CIO convention except for Patricia Harris, U.S. Secretary of Housing and Urban Development (Eaton, op. cit.).

255. Edna E. Raphael, "Working Women and Their Membership in Labor Unions," *Monthly Labor Review* 97(5):27, May 1974.

256. Herbert Hammerman and Marvin Rogoff, "The Union Role in Title VII Enforcement," *Civil Rights Digest* 7(3):22, spring 1975.

257. Ibid., p. 30.

258. For a statement of why equality is desirable, see Pamela Roby (ed.), *The Poverty Establishment*, Englewood Cliffs, N.J.: Prentice-Hall, 1974, pp. 18-21; for a description of existing inequalities, see S.M. Miller and Pamela Roby, *The Future of Inequality*, New York: Basic Books, 1970.

INDEX

Abortion, 78-79
Advocates for Women, 14
Affirmative action, 32, 58
Affirmative action programs, 23, 34, 59
AFL-CIO, 11, 59
Amalgamated Clothing and Textile Workers Union, 80
American Civil Liberties Union Foundation, 66
American Federation of Labor, 92
American Federation of State, County, and Municipal Employees (AFSCME), 33
American Health Foundation, 22
American Telephone & Telegraph Co. (A.T.&T.), 23. *See also* Affirmative action programs
Apparel manufacturing, 13
Apprenticeship, 67-70
Aronowitz, Stanley, 44
Australia, 70

Baker, Sally Hillsman, 13
Balanced Growth and Full Employment Act, 59
Beard, Rose, 88
Bell Telephone System, 23
Bemis, Stephen, 22
Bender, Marilyn, 58

Better Jobs for Women, 14
Bingham, Eula, 45
Black women, 1, 13-16, 60, 84
Black Women's Employment Program, 60
Blue-collar women. *See also* Unions
affirmative action goals, 32
filing complaints under Title VII, 23-33
history of, 1-3, 8-9
part-time work for, 53
policies affecting, 89-90
publications on, 7-8
research, 3, 8-9, 11
Blue-collar workers, 1, 7, 20, 27, 68
marriages among, 84-85
Bluestone, Barry, 54, 73,75
Bolling, Richard, 34
Briggs, Norma, 14, 41, 69
Bureau of Labor Statistics (BLS) 52, 94
Bureau of Occupational and Adult Education, 64

Carruthers, Sandy, 14
Carter, Jimmy, 36, 59
Center for the Comparative Study of Social Roles, 19-20
Center for Women and Work, 2
Chafe, William H., 54

Champagne, Joseph E., 23
Chisholm, Shirley, 67
Civil Aeronautics Board (CAB), 34
Civil Rights Act of 1964
   amendment to (1977), 77-78
   Title VII of, 31-37, 43, 46, 49-50,
      77, 96
Civil Rights Commission, 79
Cleveland Foundation, 7
Coalition of Labor Union Women
      (CLUW), 11, 33, 50, 58, 84,
      87, 89, 93, 102
Coalition of Women Truck Drivers,
      Los Angeles, 44
Commissioner of Education, 66
Commission on Working Women, 2
Committee on Labor and Public
      Welfare, Senate, 48
Communication Workers of
      America (CWA), 11
Community services, 83
Comprehensive Employment Train-
      ing Act (CETA), 68
Consciousness-raising conferences,
      42
Consumer's League, 7
Cook, Alice, 21

Department of Defense, 54, 64
Department of Health, Education
      and Welfare (DHEW), 45, 67
Department of Labor, 1, 45, 92
   and apprenticeship programs, 68
   Bureau of Labor Statistics,
      *Dictionary of Occupational
      Titles* (D.O.T.), 14, 40-41
   Employment and Earnings, 51
   funding for vocational education,
      64
   Manpower Administration,
      Office of Federal Contract
      Compliance, 31
   unemployment, statistics on, 57

unemployment insurance, recom-
      mendations on, 81
   Wage and Hour Division, 31, 33,
      39-40
   Women's Bureau, Y.W.C.A.,
      sponsor for, 14
Dictionary of Occupational Titles
      (D.O.T.) *See* Department of
      Labor
Dow Chemical Corporation, 49

Education Act Amendments of
      1976, 67
Elementary, Secondary, and Voca-
      tion Education,, House Sub-
      committee on, 67
Employment and Training Admini-
      stration, 68
Equal Credit Opportunity Act, 77
Equal Employment Opportunity
      Commission (EEOC), 22-23,
      32-33, 50, 95
   and compliance agencies, 31-32
   and Wisconsin Women in
      Apprenticeship Project, 62
   complaints in investigating, 36-37
   in arbitration cases, 95
   programs, 37
   Title VII. *See* Civil Rights Act of
      1964
Equal employment, 22-23
Equal Opportunity and Full
      Employment Act (Balanced
      Growth and Full Employment
      Act), 59
Equal Pay Act, 31, 33, 39
Exxon Corporation, 49

Federal Communications Commis-
      sion (FCC), 34
Federal Contract Compliance
      Office. *See* Department of
      Labor

Federal Power Commission (FPC), 34
Federal Reserve Board, 59, 77
Ferree, Myra Marx, 16, 18-19
Finley, Mary Lou, 16, 18
Ford Foundation, 2, 12, 21
Ford Motor Company, 88
Ford, Gerald R., 48
France, 70

General Accounting Office (GAO), 34-35
General Services Administration, 35
Gerner, Jennifer, 79
Gomez, Bitsy, 44
Griffiths, Martha, 82
Gross, Bertram, 57

Haener, Dorothy, 33
Haskins, Dorothy, 14
Hawkins, Augustus, 59
Hawthorne experiments, 9
Health insurance, 79
Health rights, 45-48. See also Occupational health
Hedges, Janice, 22
Herman, Alexis, 60
Herrick, Neal, 87
Hotel and Restaurant Employees Union, 46
Howe, Louise Kapp, 21
Huerta, Delores, 12
Human Engineering Laboratory, 38
Humphrey, Hubert H., 59
Humphrey-Hawkins bill, 59
Hungary, 78
Hunt, Vilma, 47

Industrial Relations Research Association, 10
Internal Revenue Service, 74
International Union of Electrical Workers, 11, 41, 88

International Union of Electrical, Radio, and Machine Workers, 39, 87
Interstate Commerce Commission (ICC), 34
Israel, 78

Jacoby, Robin, 21
Japan, 91
Job analysis field centers, 40
Job corps, 61, 70
Job evaluation, 39-41
Jobs Options, 62
Johnson, Gloria, 41, 58, 92
Johnson, Lyndon B., 31
    Executive Order 11246, 31, 34
    Executive Order 11375, 31
Johnson O'Connor Research Foundation, 38

Kantor, Rosabeth, 3
Kaufman, Jacob, 23,
Komarovsky, Mirra, 9, 85
Kornbluh, Joyce, 21, 69

Labor Education Advancement Program, 62
Labor force data, 1-2, 15
Labor Law Reform Act of 1977 (H.R. 8410), 91
Labor Management Relations, House Subcommittee on, 91
Labor unions. See Unions
Lamphere, Louise, 16, 19
Law enforcement process, 31
Lead Industries Association, 49
Lee, Mary Dean, 42
Lein, Laura, 16-17
Lewis, Morgan, 23,
Long-Laws, Judy, 23
Lopata, Helena Z., 19
Lordstown wildcat strike, 84
Loyola University, 20

Madar, Olga, 58
Manpower Administration, 14
Maternity benefits in Sweden and
    U.S.S.R., 50
  leave, 77-78
  provided by Government union,
    and company, 77-78
Meatcutters and Butcher Workers,
    11
Metropolitan Applied Research
    Center, 13
Meyer, Herbert, 42
Michigan, University of, 21-22, 47
  Institute for Industrial and Labor
    Relations, 69
Military training, 59-60
Mills, C. Wright, 3
Minority women, 1, 13-16, 60, 69
  See also Black women
Momma, 83
Mondale, Walter, 67
Mount Sinai Hospital, 46
Murray-Wagner Full Employment
    bill, 58-59

National Advisory Council on
    Extension and Continuing
    Education, 64
National Commission on the
    Observance of International
    Women's Year, 43, 77
National Commission on Working
    Women, 2, 102
National Congress of Neighborhood
    Women, 11, 84, 102
National Council of Jewish
    Women, 80
National Institute of Education, 2,
    64
National Institute of Mental Health
    (NIMH), 14-15, 17, 19
National Institute of Occupational
    Safety and Health (NIOSH), 48

National Labor Relations Act,
    91-92
National Organization for Women
    (NOW), 11, 58, 91
National Planning Association, 63
National Union of Hospital and
    Health Care Employees, 78
National Women's Conference, 92
Nelson, Anne, 21, 53, 70
New York City Trade Union
    Women's Program, 70
New York Triangle Shirtwaist fire,
    8
Nixon, Richard M., 48
Norton, Eleanor Holmes, 36
Nuclear Regulatory Commission
    (NRC), 49

Occupational health, 1
  and occupational diseases, 45-47
  and treatment for illnesses
    induced by chemicals, 45-46
  Occupational Safety and Health
    Act for, 48
  of pregnant workers, 45-46,
    48-49
  rights and working conditions,
    45-48
  union support for, 49-50
Occupational Safety and Health
    Act, 45-48
Occupational Safety and Health
    Administration (OSHA), 48
O'Farrell, Brigid, 23
Office of Education, U.S., 64
Office of Management and Budget,
    77
On-the-job training, 67-69

Parnes study, 14-15, 84
Perkins, Carl, 67
Perlman, Laura, 81
Philadelphia Plan, 43

Planned Parenthood Federation of America, 78
Public Health Service, 45

Rockefeller Foundation, 2, 21
Rubin, Lillian, 16-17, 83
Russell Sage Foundation, 7

Sam Houston High School. *See* Vocational education
Sandoval, Chela, 60
Schiffer, Clara, 45
Schrank, Robert, 53
Securities and Exchange Commission (SEC), 34
Seifer, Nancy, 20, 69, 90
Selikoff, Irving, 46
Sex segregation, 37-38
Sexton, Brendon, 84
Sexton, Patricia, 22, 84
Sheppard, Harold, 87
Smeal, Eleanor, 91
Social Research, Inc., 20, 87
Social security, 82
Social Security Administration, 20, 74
Society for Occupational and Environmental Health (SOEH), 45
Society for the Study of Social Problems, 2
Sociologists for Women in Society, 2
Spokeswoman, The, 49, 67
Steiger, JoAnn, 23
Stellman, Jeanne, 22
Stevenson, Mary, 22, 41, 73
Stewart, William H., 46
Supreme Court, U.S., 43, 78
Sweden, 48, 90

Tarr-Whelan, Linda, 33, 79
Title VII. *See* Civil Rights Act of 1964

Traditionally male jobs, 22, 41-43, 59, 63

Unemployment insurance, 81
Unions, 11
    formation of, 11-12
    lack of education concerning, 91
    strikes, 12, 84
    studies, 21-22
    women's membership in, 21-22, 91
Union Women's Alliance To Gain Equality (Union WAGE), 11
United Automobile Workers (UAW), 11, 33
    Women's Committee on, 88
United Electrical Workers, 87
United Farm Workers, 12
U.S.S.R., 48

Vienna, Austria, 70
Vocational education, 61-67
    counseling, 63-65
    programs, 23-24
    Sam Houston High School, model for, 23
    schools, 13
    textbooks, 65
Vocational Education Act,
Vocational Education Amendments of 1968, 64-65

Wage and Hour Division. *See* Department of Labor
Wages, 31-37, 73-77
    inequalities, 32-33
    minimum, 76
Waldman, Elizabeth, 38
Wallace, Phyllis, 13
Walshok, Mary Lindenstein, 14
Warren, Rachelle, 20, 47
Washington, D.C., subway project, 43

Weinstein, James, 8
Wertheimer, Barbara, 21, 70, 93
Wertheimer-Nelson study, 94
West Germany, 50, 70
Weyand, Ruth, 39, 87
White-collar women, 3, 20
Wisconsin, State of
    Civil Service Classification and
      Compensation Plan, 41
    Employment Service, 14
    Occupational Analysis Field
      Center, 41
    maternity leave, establishment
      of, 79
    Occupational Analysis Project, 40

Women in Apprenticeship
    Project, 61, 69
Witt, Mary, 41
Wolfbein, Seymour, 58
Wolfgang, Myra, 46
Women's Bureau, 7, 60
Women's liberation movement, 12,
    16-17
Women's Right Project, 66
Women's vocational education bills,
    67
Work Incentive Program (WIN),
    61, 68, 70

Young, Marilyn, 21
YWCA, 7, 14